OCT   2007

GAME OF MY LIFE:
OHIO
STATE

MEMORABLE STORIES OF BUCKEYE FOOTBALL

STEVE GREENBERG
AND LAURA LANESE

SP
SPORTS
PUBLISHING
L.L.C.

SportsPublishingLLC.com

ISBN 10: 1-58261-821-6
ISBN 13: 978-1-58261-821-0

Publishers: Peter L. Bannon and Joseph J. Bannon Sr.
Senior managing editor: Susan M. Moyer
Acquisitions editor: Mike Pearson
Developmental editor: Travis Moran
Art director: K. Jeffrey Higgerson
Dust jacket design: Heidi Norsen
Interior layout: Heidi Norsen
Photo editor: Erin Linden-Levy

Sports Publishing L.L.C.
804 North Neil Street
Champaign, IL 61820
Phone: 1-877-424-2665
Fax: 217-363-2073
SportsPublishingLLC.com

Printed in the United States of America

Library of Congress Cataloging-in-Publication Data

Greenberg, Steve, 1956-
  Game of my life : Ohio State memorable stories of Buckeye football
/ Steve Greenberg with Laura Lanese.
    p. cm.
  Includes bibliographical references.
  ISBN-13: 978-1-58261-821-0 (hard cover : alk. paper)
  ISBN-10: 1-58261-821-6 (hard cover : alk. paper)
  1. Ohio State University--Football--History. 2. Ohio State Buckeyes
(Football team)--History.   I. Lanese, Laura. II. Title.
GV958.O35G75 2006
796.332'630977157--dc22
                              2006023881

For my mother, Joanie, the best damned quarterback. Ever.
—SG

To my husband, Mike, now I wish I knew you when—and to
my children, Michael, Camille, and Francesca, may you all
have a game of your life.
And finally, to my mom … just because.
—LBL

CONTENTS

AUTHORS' NOTES

BY STEVE GREENBERG

To suggest that there have been many standout performances within the storied football history at The Ohio State University is a grave understatement. That's what this book is about, though, and thank you for buying it, because that makes my mom proud of me ... even if I didn't become a doctor.

Maybe these phenomenal feats have lulled us all into great expectations when considering OSU football. We sit in Ohio Stadium—or we watch on television—really believing that *this game* is the one where a particular player will write or rewrite history. We do that because we are passionate about many things on Saturdays in the fall, and because we all believe we are lay experts on the Scarlet and Gray. Therefore, we not only are empowered to make such bold proclamations, but we actually believe the statements we make.

Really, what we're doing is issuing opinions, nothing more, and nothing less. We don't coach—well, at least not on the field or from the press box. We certainly don't play—although we offer utterances like, "I could've run through that hole. ..." and equally dim-witted observations. No, we predict. We study matchups: this wide receiver versus that cornerback, this fullback versus that linebacker, and so on. We're sure we have it down—so much so, in fact, that when we open our mouths and let the words of wisdom drip, we expect everyone around us to stand, if not salute, in reverence of our awesome expertise.

And so to those among us who suggest, "Why don't you get a life?" and offer that there is more to our mortal existence than six or seven home games a year and, cash permitting, a few road trips and a bowl game—we offer this quintessential retort:

"Oh, *yeah?*"

You're probably wondering where this is leading. Be still—our book, our rules.

Back in 1972, on a gray September afternoon (sorry, Grantland Rice), I sat in Ohio Stadium with my dad, a buddy, and his dad. Being from Bexley, on the eastside of Columbus, we always kept tabs on neighboring Eastmoor High School. There was a kid, about my age, who'd become a figurative lethal weapon as a running back. We'd follow his progress, either in person or in the pages of the now late, great *Columbus Citizen-Journal*.

The week before this sortie to the stadium, I watched as Woody Hayes cleared the bench late in a 55-13 thrashing of Iowa in the season-opener. To the best of my recollection, the kid we'd all followed in high school, in his customary tiptoe gait, took the field with the rest of the AYOs (all you others) to close out the victory. I expected more from Archie Griffin—*way* more. He was just months removed from tearing apart some damned good Central Ohio opponents, and now this, an AYO? Certainly, he would work his swivel-hipped magic against the scrubs from Iowa. I said exactly that to my dad, who passively shrugged his shoulders, probably planning a quick getaway to avoid being mired in the massive traffic mismanagement of the day.

The jaws of wisdom began to drip. "Watch this, Pop—he'll bust this one and go all the way." Another passive shrug. As those who know me well will tell you, I'm *always* right, except for those rare occurrences when I could possibly be considered, uh … not right. *Always!* To prove my point, the ball was snapped deep in OSU territory at the north end of the field. The quarterback wheeled, and handed the ball to Griffin, who began the race downfield.

Or was it? Nope. Fumble … change of possession … game over— one carry, one fumble.

"It's a ploy," I told my dad. "I'll bet Woody had him do that to distract North Carolina [the next opponent]." Insert third passive shrug here. North Carolina? Did I just say that? Hindsight being the perfect tool, I am now compelled to state without fear of contradiction that I think I'd had too many stadium 'dogs by that point. Clearly, I was affected.

Most of us know the next chapter of the story: Archie was forced to carry a football with him the next week—every single day, nearly every single minute. Woody didn't want him to forget, and he certainly didn't want him to fumble again.

Now for the denouement—the next week against the Tar Heels, OSU was trailing, 7-0, in the first half. The OSU crowd was sitting on its hands, which, sadly, was often the case. The Buckeyes were sluggish at best. See, this figured to be one of those games where they just rolled the ball out onto the field and the home team won by about 50 points. About 32 ardent UNC fans were nearing a collective aneurysm as the vaunted Buckeyes were stalled time and time again. They *believe*, those UNC fans. They're certain their Tar Heels will pull off this week's upset of the century.

What the three dozen North Carolina fans didn't know was what ... well, *I* knew. OSU had the secret weapon from Eastmoor. Already a household name as a result of his prep career, No. 45 was about to make his mark. I told that to my dad, my buddy, and his dad. When the announcer said, "Offensive substitution—Griffin in for ... [whomever]," the stadium came alive—in a way. All of a sudden, the bluebloods weren't sitting on their hands anymore. It's not that they were overtly cheering, either. There were some golf claps, but this act was more a craning of curiosity. Griffin? You mean the kid from Eastmoor? A freshman? Has Woody lost it? Woody doesn't play freshmen, does he?

Yes—especially on that day.

Buckeye Nation knows how this one turned out. Griffin ran for a then-school record 239 yards, and the hometown heroes cleaned up their act enough to warrant a 29-14 victory.

Columbus had a new icon, and I, the fervent follower of OSU football, had the game of my life—in drips of wisdom, I mean. Not being one to say, "I told you so," I told you so.

So that's my game, and you know the reasons why—which really doesn't matter, because I never wore the Scarlet and Gray. What does matter is that, of the former players who participated in this project, each has his distinctive reason for choosing a particular game. Some you would expect, some you wouldn't—it boils down to personal choice.

Is this a great country, or what?

It's another trip down Memory Lane. Let them show you the way.

—SG

I'm afraid to admit this in print, but I used to find the fascination with Ohio State football somewhat amusing and, yes, even slightly annoying. I did my undergrad at Miami of Ohio, where we had first claim to Woody and Bo, and where students could go to their football games free. Then I went to Ohio State for graduate school, where on autumn Saturdays I suffered through traffic, crowds, and revelers gone wild on my front lawn. "It's just football," I used to think, not quite appreciating the unprincipled nature of my heresy.

Fast-forward several years, and I'm an Ohio State law school alum and wife of a former player. My attitude toward Buckeye football has softened a little over the years. But when Steve offered me the opportunity to co-author this book, I wasn't quite sure I could represent the players as well as an "I bleed scarlet and gray" fan.

After working on this book, though, I can now say I get it. Interviewing this amazing group of guys has been an eye-opening experience. Story after story, I was impressed by the hard work, the dedication, and the character building that goes into making an Ohio State football player. Some were only a few years removed from the game, some many decades. But they all remembered with surprising clarity the detail and subtlety of the moment. Uniformly, they praised the tenacity of their teammates, the commitment of their coaches, the encouragement of the fans, and the honor they felt playing for the Buckeyes.

This is a behind-the-scenes look at the great moments in the history of Ohio State football. But it's really much more than that. It's the story of talented athletes practicing their craft with love and passion, not just for the game, but for their school, their teammates, and their families as well. The Ohio State community should be proud of its contribution to the great tradition of Buckeye football—on and off the field. These athletes are articulate, helpful, funny, humble, and gracious. I can only hope that the following pages do justice to their stories.

—LBL

ACKNOWLEDGMENTS

BY STEVE GREENBERG

Were it not for the cooperation of the players profiled in the following pages, this book would not exist. It's not enough to say "thank you" to these Buckeye greats, but that's what we offer—gratitude for opening up and reliving the definitive glory days of their careers.

This project never occurred to me, which is why I have Mike Pearson, acquisitions editor extraordinaire at Sports Publishing LLC to similarly thank. Mike called me and pitched the notion of me doing the book. I told him I would need to think about it, which I did ... for about three seconds. Inasmuch as we all re-live facets of our lives, being able to help former OSU football greats do the same was another rare treat. Yes, I'm a fan, and don't expect an apology. Travis Moran of SP did yeoman's work in helping get this book to market—thank you, sir.

Laura Lanese, you're an author! You have no idea how much it means to me that you decided to throw in on this. Were it not for you, I'd still be smiling and dialing, and Pearson would be wondering, "Where in the hell is Greenberg's book?" It has been a pleasure, kiddo, and it will happen again! (Everyone everywhere: Laura will become a noted author in the not-too-distant future. The ink already is in her veins.)

Mike Eads, fortunately for us, still had eligibility remaining, so we suited him up as a contributing editor. (He's quite good at it, too; the guy edits a newspaper by day and "gets" deadlines. Forgive him, please, for being an Indiana University supporter.)

This is the part where I'm supposed to thank my wife, Sally, and my daughters, Annie and Rachel, for their unflagging patience while I wrote this book—except they're always all so busy going in different directions that I don't think they noticed. Thanks, Chix, Inc., my very own "atoms in a blender." I love you.

And then there are the usual suspects, the folks who sit back and simply wonder with raised eyebrows (I'm not sure how to take that) when I tell them another book is on the way.

That means: Thanks to Sparky and the crew of the SV *shimeshay'n* for yet another lovely cruise; to Tomi Tsumani and Dr. John for the musical encouragement (which had nothing whatsoever to do with the writing of this book); to The Mogul, whose shared penchant for unbridled entrepreneurship means only good things to come; to Patty Lee, "G", and P.T., who, independently, are having the games of their lives, and, of course, to all the good folks at Peninsula Paving for keeping the ride smooth.

Steve Greenberg
June 1, 2006
Carmel, Indiana

BY LAURA LANESE

I gratefully acknowledge all the players who gave up their time to share their stories and their humor with unbelievable modesty. Thanks to Mike for being such an amazing writer that I was able to get this project by default—and to Steve, thanks for the opportunity to uncover my inner Buckeye.

Laura Lanese
June 1, 2006
Grove City, Ohio

A.J. HAWK

BIRTH DATE: January 6, 1984
HOMETOWN: Centerville, Ohio
RESIDENCE: Green Bay, Wisconsin
HEIGHT: 6-foot-1
WEIGHT: 240 pounds
POSITION: Linebacker
YEARS: 2002 to 2005

Hawk was named male Athlete of the Year at Ohio State for 2006 ... Perennial all-Big Ten linebacker, consensus All-America, Lombardi Award winner, Butkus Award winner ... All-state in high school ... Humble and soft-spoken. ... He was the Most Valuable Player on 2005's Ohio State football team that finished 10-2 and shared the Big Ten championship.

The Run-up

A.J. Hawk knew Sun Devil Stadium well. This would be his third Fiesta Bowl there, the more famous being the national championship won there against Miami in January 2003. There's another reason Hawk knew the nuances of that field, the history forever embedded in its turf: Pat Tillman.

Tillman was the former Arizona State All-America linebacker who went on to star in the NFL for the Arizona Cardinals ... on this same field. Then, possibly the most mobile linebacker who would hit as hard as a proverbial ton of bricks simply walked away in his prime. No amount of money could keep him pinned to the Cardinals' roster. He had a higher calling: defending the United States from the throes of terrorism. So Tillman, Hawk's role model on the field, enlisted in the U.S. Army Rangers, ultimately being called to duty in Afghanistan. Sadly, he was killed by friendly fire.

So it was with a knowing mind that Hawk, his mane flowing from beneath his helmet—just as Tillman's once did—took to Sun Devil Stadium for the third and most important time. Substitute the No. 47 of Hawk for the No. 44 of Tillman, and one couldn't be called crazy if Hawk were his reincarnation.

Quick side note: In tribute to Tillman, his accomplishments, and service to his country, Hawk and his fellow starting linebackers, Bobby Carpenter and Anthony Schlegel, let their hair grow ... and grow—and then some. It was their way to pay homage to the man who played the game the only way he knew how—full force, which is what often is said of Hawk.

Yet another subplot of this Fiesta Bowl was the constant glare of the media spotlight on, of all things, Hawk's engagement to Laura Quinn—sister of Notre Dame quarterback Brady Quinn—as if it mattered. But Hawk smiled his way through every inane question about the relationship, then went out and proceeded to pound the living tar out of the man who would one day become his brother-in-law.

A.J. Hawk says the Fiesta Bowl was the end of "an amazing four years."

Hawk remembers the weather as "Arizona-perfect, about 78 degrees and sunny" and the stadium was "full." That's a bit of an understatement. If the sea of humanity wanted to, it could have bent back the light towers to create a little breathing room. And although OSU was wearing its "away whites" as the visiting team, this amounted to something of a home game for the Buckeyes—kind of like when they play Indiana University in Bloomington—given the huge contingent of Ohio State alumni living in the greater Phoenix area. Besides, as all the bowl-organizing committees across the nation know, Ohio State "travels" very well.

With all that good-natured hell-raising going on in the stands before the game, it was business as usual down on the field. "We tried to keep things as normal as we could in warmups but we [the seniors] all knew this was our last game together, and it was important to get the job done," Hawk explained. "We kept to our routines as we did all season. It was good to see Bobby [Carpenter] go through warmups with us, after his Michigan game injury, but we pretty much knew he wouldn't be able to play in the game. The crowd was great ... much scarlet in the stadium. My family was seated in the front row."

It's a question of curiosity: "A.J., what was your greatest game?"

"People ask me all the time for 'the best ... the best game, the best play, my favorite hit, play, game, teammate.' I have a very hard time giving *just one*. I love everything about Ohio State—that is why it is so hard to boil an amazing experience down to a game or a play," he said, before yielding to the Fiesta Bowl of his senior season. "That said, when I think about some of the biggest moments, they go something like this: The national championship game [31-24, double overtime against Miami] my freshman year was clearly the greatest team accomplishment. We will always be 'the national championship team.' That is a great feeling. Save for special teams plus a handful of plays from scrimmage, I was not a huge contributor to that game. Our seniors led the way.

"It is awfully hard to top the experience of my last game in the Horseshoe [Ohio Stadium]—Senior Day, when we played Northwestern, which beat us the year before up in Evanston. It was so amazing to see our great senior class run out there, one by one, first to

Coach Tressel, then to our parents. It was pretty special being the last senior announced, following my friend, roommate, and youth-football teammate [center] Nick Mangold out on the field. That was a game full of fun emotions as we played great, got the job done, then had the chance to leave the game one by one for one last celebration in the 'Shoe."

But then there was the Tussle in Tempe. Beating Notre Dame, 34-20, in the Arizona desert was what Hawk and his teammates had to do. So, there was Hawk making sacks. There was Hawk busting up double-teams. And over there was Hawk, foiling a pass attempt. And, oh, yeah, there was Hawk drilling yet another running back into the grass.

The Game

By A.J. Hawk

Ohio State vs. Notre Dame
The Fiesta Bowl—January 2, 2006

I think the fact that, because it was the end of an amazing four years—four big bowl wins, three Michigan wins, *lots* of victories in those four years—and an amazing group of teammates and coaches is why it felt like the game of my life.

There also were other factors such as Notre Dame being the opponent; Brady Quinn being the opposing quarterback; and all the talk of Charlie Weis (the former New England Patriots assistant head coach in his first year at the Irish helm) having over a month to prepare. I would later say, after the win, that Coach (Jim) Tressel deserved the same credit in that he prepared us well to win four bowl games in a row.

We then went out and got the job done, despite an early Notre Dame touchdown and some OSU turnovers; we overcame any adversity and played a great game.

I was constantly asked all week if I would be able to go my hardest against Brady, given the family connection. I pretty consistently said that would not be a problem, that I would go hard against my own brother, Ryan (who is also a great quarterback). My future fiancée, Laura, wondered who she should root for, and she even had a special jersey that was half Brady's Notre Dame No. 10 and half my Ohio State No. 47. I told her all along that she had to root for her brother—that she had been with him all her life; she could root for me *after* the Fiesta Bowl.

Fortunately, despite some early things that went wrong, we really got rolling, connecting on some big offensive plays—(quarterback) Troy Smith, (and receivers) Teddy Ginn, and Anthony (Gonzales), and the guys really stood out that day—and we settled down and played a great defensive game after the first series when Notre Dame scored. I even had a couple of sacks of Brady. I've signed quite a few pictures taken that day; some people even ask Brady to sign them next to my name.

The Aftermath

Hawk took every opportunity to soak in what he and his teammates had just accomplished. With the NFL draft just three and a half months away, he knew this was the end of the Ohio State road—although once a Buckeye, always a Buckeye. Still, it was the end of a great run.

"I was very, very happy for our whole group—the coaches and my teammates and myself," Hawk said. "All of those seniors on that podium were so happy. I spoke with as many people as I could on the field. You can never be completely satisfied in a game, but I was really happy that we got the job done.

"At the press conference after the game, I was ready to say what had been on my mind for a while—I wanted to address all the 'If you give Charlie a month to prepare, he'll beat you,' talk with some talk about a man that was very special to me and my teammates—Jim Tressel. I said that Coach Tressel was the ultimate Big Game Coach. I said to look at what *he* does when he gets a month to prepare. I played in four bowl games with Coach and we won *all four* times. I played in four Michigan games with Coach, and we won three of them.

"We beat some great teams in my four-year career, and I wanted our great team and more importantly our unbelievable coaching staff to get the credit that they deserved," Hawk asserted. "I can't name them all here, but I must mention Luke Fickell, the best position coach anyone could hope for, who means a lot to me. Coach Jim Heacock ... I'll never forget how emotional he was in speaking on my behalf at the Butkus Award night, and he was an unbelievable defensive coordinator, who prepares like crazy and really brought aggressiveness to the team. Butch Reynolds was a great addition; he taught me so much, and I really will always remember that, despite being a legitimate world superstar himself in track. He really loves being a part of the OSU football team."

After showering, dressing, and departing the stadium, Hawk got together with family and friends, about 20 of them, "... at a nice steakhouse in Phoenix for a late dinner. I realized that night that I was an alum—a 'former' Buckeye football player. It was time to move on to the next phase of my life—graduation, the NFL draft, and hopefully, continuing to represent Ohio State always. I, as Coach Tressel said, started focusing on 'what's next.'"

Still, as much as the game meant to him, Hawk is reluctant to call it his greatest achievement overall.

"I honestly can't point to a greatest accomplishment," he said. "I often look at the [North Carolina] State overtime victory we had earlier in my career as a game that might have been the toughest win we had as a group. I think those three Michigan wins probably are the greatest team accomplishment. I have a hard time pointing to an individual 'greatest accomplishment.' The work of a linebacker is more of a complete body of work than any one game. I just really like that Notre Dame game the best, because it was such a perfect ending for so many of us."

If the ending were perfect, the beginning could be considered just as idyllic. Hawk began playing in the second grade, and he hasn't looked back.

"Growing up as a kid in Ohio playing football, we all dreamed of playing for Ohio State," he said. "They started showing interest early in my junior year. I was offered scholarships by other schools earlier, but when Ohio State offered me a scholarship in June 2001, the summer before my senior year in high school, I accepted after thinking about it for just one week. It could not have worked out better.

"I had a great childhood that was full of sports, my two older brothers, and friends. We played all sports—baseball, basketball [I thought in the early days that I would grow up to play point guard for Duke], football, track, swimming," Hawk continued. "I loved my high school career, especially my freshman and sophomore years, when I got to play side by side with my brother, Ryan, who I still think might be the best player I've ever been around. We had an awesome team at Centerville with amazing coaches. I still go back there often to be around those coaches. My oldest brother, Matt, was the first to go through the incredible Centerville football program. He led the way for Ryan and me. My life growing up was great—I felt I was in the perfect place."

Hawk said in basketball he was fortunate to play on travel teams (*You* want to guard him?) that won several national championships.

"Several players from that team went on to play [NCAA] Division-I sports. I really liked baseball. I pitched, played shortstop and outfield. I swam when I was young—all the strokes. My brother, Ryan, and I would play tennis for hours at a court near our house. We had long, loud matches."

Hawk's parents still live in Centerville, and he said they and other family members have shown the utmost in support. His tennis nemesis, Ryan, is in the Arena Football League, and his other brother, Matt, is "an electrician who can fix anything. He and his wife, Beth, have two great kids, my nephew, Nathan, and my niece, Paige. My grandparents, Dean and Mary Hawk, and Aunt Kim, and my grandmother, Georgie Poeppelman, all are around us, and they love our football."

When he's not preparing to shred, or actually is shredding, opposing offensive schemes, Hawk relishes his down time. "I like to hunt when I can with my old homeroom teacher at Centerville, Mr.

Dillman. I follow my brother Ryan's football career as closely as I can. We play golf, relax, workout, and read."

When all is said and done, and the cleats are hung up for the final time, Hawk said he prefers to be remembered not for his individual talents, which are many. Just mark him down as "… a good teammate, who was on great teams that won a lot, as a player who always gave everything he had, as a player who could be relied upon."

Appreciative of the road traveled and the people who helped him along the way, Hawk isn't likely to forget. "I will always refer back to my days as a Buckeye, just as I still refer back to my high school days at Centerville. I learned so many things, met so many fantastic people, and grew from an 18-year-old, who wondered where and how I would fit in, to a 21-year-old who had an amazing experience.

"Though my NFL career has taken me to Green Bay, my new home, I will always return to Columbus and to Ohio State," Hawk nodded fondly. "I hope I have the good fortune to have a good career in the NFL. I plan on living someday in Columbus when my playing days are over. It's the place in the world I love the most."

2

ARCHIE GRIFFIN

BIRTH DATE: August 21, 1954
HOMETOWN: Columbus, Ohio
RESIDENCE: Westerville, Ohio
POSITION: Tailback
HEIGHT: 5-foot-9
WEIGHT: 182 pounds
YEARS: 1972 to 1975

A perennial All-Big Ten selection and the Chicago Tribune *Player of the Year, as well as a multi-time All-American and two-time Heisman Trophy winner, Griffin was the co-Ohio High School Back of the Year as a senior at Eastmoor High School. He also was all-state, all-district (as a junior and as a senior), All-City (as a junior and as a senior) and Sunkist All-America. "Mainly, I played fullback, and occasionally cornerback," Griffin said. "I ran track—the 400-meter and 800-meter relays and threw a little shot put and wrestled [167 pounds]. ..." He played with Cincinnati in the NFL and Jacksonville in the USFL. Formerly an associate director of athletics at OSU, he now runs the school's alumni association.*

The Run-up

Game day dawned overcast and just a bit cool. It was odd for late September in Columbus, but it was Football Saturday, and regardless of the weather, "war" was at hand.

Entering the game, no one knew what to expect of this Ohio State team. Not that North Carolina was a shoo-in for the national championship. The more pertinent question was whether an inspired group of Buckeyes would show up against the Atlantic Coast Conference's best team.

Columbus native Archie Griffin remembered the setting easily.

"It was a full stadium," he said. "The capacity at the time was 86,000, and we were at capacity."

Some would suggest "beyond capacity."

"The night before the game, the varsity spent the night at the hotel, while the freshman reserves stayed in the dormitory and met the rest of the team at the stadium," Griffin continued. "There were a few of us freshmen who went to the hotel before the game and met with the position coaches. And then we rode over [to Ohio Stadium] with the team on the bus.

"The coaches went over the game plan and talked about the plays we were going to run. You listened to everything Coach [Woody] Hayes said, especially as a freshman. I still had no idea that I was going to get an opportunity to play. I just paid attention to all the things he said. He usually talked about not making mistakes, about securing the ball from a running-back standpoint, taking care of the little things so that the big things would take care of themselves."

On this day, Archie Griffin would forever become a household name—in Columbus, across the nation and beyond our borders.

"This was the game that put me on the map," Griffin said in something of an understatement. "I had no idea I would get in the game. I wasn't expecting to play at all, and then to be able to break a [single-game] record is what makes this the game of my life. The game before against Iowa, I got in the game for one play and fumbled the football. I was taken out of the game after that. I had heard all the stories about guys fumbling the ball and never getting a chance to play again at Ohio State, especially being a freshman. At the time, there were a lot of Division I coaches who didn't think freshmen were ready to play Division I football. This was the first year that freshmen were eligible to play on varsity."

Hayes wasn't exactly hell-bent to get Griffin into the game. His position on freshmen, previously, was that the best thing about them was that they ultimately would become sophomores. But Griffin had a "guardian angel" on this day.

The Game

By Archie Griffin

North Carolina at Ohio State—September 30, 1972

North Carolina blocked a punt and went ahead of us 7-0 in the first quarter. To get in after that really surprised me. I was so surprised that I almost forgot my helmet when they called my name. I couldn't believe they were calling my name. All week in practice, I had practiced on the scout squad, not for varsity. It was truly a miracle. I really wanted to play bad, and I remember praying the night before for the opportunity to get a chance.

I remember my first play when I came off the bench was an off tackle. I probably gained five or six yards on it. That whole day was a blur. I remember [defensive back] Steve Luke telling me, "Run like you've never run before." They told me my eyes were wide open throughout the whole game, like I was in a daze. Thank goodness I knew the plays. I do remember a bit. I remember running a lot of off-tackle plays. I remember scoring a touchdown on a 19 sweep— running to the left side, I think, in the last series I played, in the middle of the fourth quarter. I remember the plays because we ran those for years, but I can't tell you what plays were called for me to run that day. All I know is they were called, and I was running them.

I think I got the ball a lot because we had success early, and coaches usually stick with what works. I'd always had a lot of confidence in our offensive linemen; they were outstanding. They did

Archie Griffin on his effort against North Carolina: "This was the game that put me on the map."

a good job of opening up the holes, and the plays were working. After the half I wasn't sure if I was supposed to go back on the field. I had to ask the coach if I was supposed to go back in the game. The whole scenario was a surprise. I didn't think I would get another shot that soon. I thought I might get a shot again during spring practice.

I later learned that our running backs coach, Rudy Hubbard, had persuaded Coach Hayes to let me get into the game. Coach Hayes had this saying that to get something you really wanted, you had to "pound the table" to get it. That is, you had to put your job on the line. My understanding was that Coach Hubbard was willing to "pound the table" for me to get into the game at that time—and then good things happened after that.

I had rushed for 239 yards that game, which set a record. I don't remember much of the specifics of the game. It felt like an out-of-body experience. I was in Ohio Stadium in front of all of these people. I was someone who had just come out of high school and playing in this big game against North Carolina. At the end of the game, when I came out, the announcers had announced that I had broken Ollie Cline's rushing record. That never occurred to me that I was on the verge of breaking a record.

OSU won, 29-14. It seemed like more, but it didn't matter—a legend was born that day.

The Aftermath

The locker room was a scene of unbridled jubilation, if not appreciation, Griffin recalls.

"Guys were grabbing me and hugging me," he said. "A lot of people were in disbelief. Champ Henson grabbed me and kissed me on the top of my head. I was pretty emotional about it. It was a wonderful feeling, being a freshman and having fumbled the previous game, then having the opportunity to play again. Having that kind of result was an amazing feeling.

"Coach Hayes congratulated us on the win. He let us know we were playing a good football team. I think that was the only game that North Carolina lost that year. And he congratulated me on the game that I had, along with the outstanding blocking I did. He always did a great job of congratulating guys on their performance. I remember watching the film on Sunday, and he told me that I might not ever have another game like [that] in my lifetime. He gave me about six or seven Buckeye leaves for that particular performance. That meant the world to me.

"After the game, some of my friends from high school came by the dorm room, and we were talking about the game. They were really proud because ABC had mentioned my name on TV, but they confused it, calling me 'Archie Greene,' probably confusing it with Cornelius Greene," Griffin chuckled. "But my friends were really proud—especially since at that time, there weren't many Columbus kids who were on Ohio State's team. So that made it special. I remember listening to the radio while I was driving and hearing them mention the record. It was a really good feeling to hear that. And to recognize that it was a miracle for me, especially because the linemen did their great job of blocking for me."

The adulation would have continued well into the night had anyone told Griffin a television appearance was next. No one bothered.

"I missed going to *The Woody Hayes Show*. I wasn't familiar how that whole thing worked," he said. "I found out later that they wanted me on the show that night. But, because no one said anything to me, I went to a concert at Mershon [Auditorium] with a friend of mine instead."

Practice for the next game came along, and Griffin said he was a man without a figurative address.

"When I went back to practice, I wasn't sure if I was supposed to line up with the first team or not," he said. "I got back into my normal position until the coaches told me to line up with the rest of the starters. From that point on, I felt like I was on that varsity, felt like I was going to be the guy playing a lot of tailback."

As a result of numerous honors Griffin garnered while at OSU, to say that his coming-out party against North Carolina was his greatest overall accomplishment as a Buckeye is very difficult.

"Certainly winning the [Heisman Trophy twice—the only one to do so] were great accomplishments, but I'd have to say that the choice I made to come to Ohio State, I think, in itself was probably the best accomplishment," he said. "I was in the right place at the right time to make all those things happen. I mean, the right coaches and the right players. I don't care how great of a player you are if you're not on a great team, it's going to be hard to have those great things happen for you, like what happened to me—as far as the North Carolina game, as far as rushing for 100 yards in over 31 straight games, and winning a couple of Heisman trophies. If you're not with a good group of people, though, those things are not going to happen."

Griffin's older brothers were at out-of-town colleges, when it came time for him to select his choice for higher education.

"It would make it easier on my parents to watch everyone play if I came to school at Ohio State, then they would only have to come across town to watch me play," he said, typically selfless. "Also, with Coach Woody Hayes, Coach Rudy Hubbard, and Coach Esco Sarkkinen, I developed a pretty good relationship. They made me feel like I could have some success at Ohio State."

Today, Griffin is the president and CEO of the Ohio State Alumni Association. "I've [also] got the Archie Griffin Scholarship fund to raise money for the Olympic sports at Ohio State in a time when a lot of schools have dropped men's sports," he said. "So we created an endowment to help Olympic sports to keep Ohio State with a large sports program. Right now, Ohio State has 36 sports, which is the largest number in the country for a Division I school.

"The Archie and Bonita Griffin scholarship fund helps children's programs in Central Ohio," Griffin explained. "We try to help children achieve the things they want to achieve, be it academics or athletics."

Griffin and Bonita have three sons, Anthony and Andre who are grown, and Adam, who at 14 is keeping his parents "really busy."

When he has the time, he'll go out and spoil a good walk, as the saying goes.

"Golf is something I've taken a liking to, although I could use a lot more work at it," he said. "I really enjoy playing it. Most of my [spare] time is following around my youngster, Adam, who participates in football, basketball, and other youth programs."

Griffin said he would prefer to be remembered as "a guy who did the best he could with what he had."

"I worked as hard as anybody in any game," Griffin asserted. "I love the game and the lessons that I learned from the game. Football was a vehicle I used to get the college education that I wanted. It was important to me because of that. Coming from a large family—six brothers and a sister—my parents couldn't afford to send eight kids to school. I knew if I was good enough in the game, I could get that scholarship to go to college. So football was something that helped me to achieve that goal."

3

MIKE LANESE

BIRTH DATE: July 6, 1964
HOMETOWN: Mayfield, Ohio
RESIDENCE: Grove City, Ohio
POSITION: Flanker
HEIGHT: 6 feet
WEIGHT: 185 pounds
YEARS: 1982 to 1986

Lanese was captain of 1985 team ... Two-time Academic All-American ... Toyota Leader of the Year ... Chevrolet MVP vs. Michigan in 1984 ... First team All-Ohio, Greater Cleveland Conference MVP, first team All-Scholastic, Lou Groza Award Winner and Northeast Ohio Back of the Year as a senior at Mayfield High School. ... His OSU position coach was Jim Tressel, now the head coach of the Buckeyes. ... Was named one of 32 U.S. Rhodes Scholars in 1986, and he studied philosophy, politics, and economics for two years at Worcester College, Oxford University. ... A free agent with the Cleveland Browns in 1988, he also served as a Surface Warfare Officer in the U.S. Navy from 1989 to 1993. Lanese is the CEO of ClearSaleing, Inc., an advertising technology company based in Dublin, Ohio.

The Run-up

"Every man is entitled to be valued by his best moment."
—Ralph Waldo Emerson

"The great thing about football is that when you get knocked down, you get up and go again."
—Woody Hayes and Earle Bruce

Throughout the history of the Ohio State-Michigan rivalry, educated and civilized commentators on both sides often have waxed poetic about the deep, enduring respect and admiration they had for each other's program. For me, not so much. Call me a cad for saying so, but I've really never cared much for anything that's come out of Michigan. Despite nearly committing to Bo Schembechler as a 17-year-old recruit, I'm pretty certain I've never liked Michigan. Even growing up in the Wolverine-friendly Cleveland area, I knew I didn't like Michigan before I'd even watched my first college football game. In fact, looking back, I can't remember ever feeling anything but contempt for Michigan, including their players, their school, their fans, and their song—especially their song.

Against this background, it should come as no surprise that the game of my life involved Michigan. It was 1984. Ronald Reagan had just been re-elected president in a landslide. Apple had revolutionized personal computing with the introduction of the Macintosh. Madonna had made a significant contribution to the end of Western civilization with her release of "Like a Virgin." I was a 20-year-old, junior flanker on the Ohio State football team.

In spite of incredible talent on that team, including legends such as Keith Byars, Cris Carter, Pepper Johnson, and Jim Lachey, we'd managed to lose two games that year. One was a heartbreaker to Purdue and the other was a sleeper to Wisconsin. There were whispers in Columbus about another underperforming season followed by a Holiday Bowl consolation prize. But thanks to a one-point Iowa loss against Michigan State, we were still in contention for an outright Big

Ten championship and a trip to Ohio State's first Rose Bowl since 1979. All we had to do was beat a mediocre Michigan team that had sputtered to a disappointing 6-4 record coming into the game. As the cliché goes, though, records don't matter in The Game. Michigan desperately wanted to salvage an off-year with a win.

The Game

By Mike Lanese

Michigan at Ohio State—November 17, 1984

At Ohio Stadium, in the 81st meeting between Michigan and Ohio State, Earle Bruce, a great coach who never got the breaks or respect he deserved, put together a surprising game plan. Instead of sticking to tradition and playing the Michigan game conservatively, Earle came out throwing. The plan might not have measured up to that of a modern West Coast offense, but in a game usually characterized by the cautious baseline play of tennis, waiting for your opponent to commit an unforced error, this was the equivalent of coming to the net. He also ran our quarterback, Mike Tomczak, on the option. We'd always had the option in our arsenal, but Tomczak had broken his leg in the spring game eight months earlier. He'd run sparingly all season, and no one expected Earle to feature him so prominently on the ground.

We moved the ball effectively in the first quarter and scored on an efficient drive. I caught a couple of balls on curl routes, the second of which put us close to the end zone. Unfortunately, at the end of the first quarter Byars re-injured an ankle he'd sprained in the Wisconsin game a few weeks earlier, and we started to get sloppy on offense. But Michigan couldn't capitalize. Its offense couldn't seem to find an attack that could generate first downs. As the second quarter started to wind down, we found ourselves struggling, but held a decisive advantage in having points on the board. With twenty-two seconds to play in the half, Michigan lined up to punt the ball from its 44-yard

First the fumble, then this catch—Mike Lanese's acrobatic reception turned the tide against Michigan.

line. We were ready to go into the locker room with a 7-0 lead and the psychological edge.

I was the punt returner. All I had to do was fair catch the ball and then we'd probably take a knee, run out the clock, and get some Gatorade. And that's when the idea hit me. They were expecting us to fair catch the ball, take a knee, run out the clock, and get some Gatorade. I remember watching the Michigan punt team and thinking that if I could catch them sleeping and get by the first few guys, I just might be able to surprise them with a big return. Even though I hadn't returned a punt for a touchdown all year, I just needed a step or two, and then it was off to the races. After all, I was faster than Cris Carter. What's the worst that could happen? Fumble? I never fumbled.

So I didn't raise my right arm to signal a fair catch. Instead, I caught the ball on our own 12-yard line, stepped right, and evaded number 33 with a spin move to the inside. Then number 37 ran by and slapped at the ball with his right hand. And I fumbled. I fumbled—in the Michigan game—with the Big Ten championship and Rose Bowl on the line.

So naturally, my only thought at that point, like any sane player in that situation, was to sneak back to the sideline without giving Earle a chance to grab me. That plan failed as well. Years later, I forget Earle's exact phrase when he caught up to me, but I'm pretty sure I could figure it out without buying any vowels.

As I watched the Michigan offense take the field, I anxiously waited for the consequence of my stupidity to manifest itself in front of 90,000 fans in the stadium and millions at home. Then, as if in some bizarre delayed reaction, about two minutes too late, I found myself working through the other side of my boneheaded decision. "On the other hand," I said to myself, "I've never returned a punt for a touchdown—not even in high school. My blockers might be sleeping, too. Cris Carter is slow. I'm really thirsty. And yes, I could fumble. In the Michigan game. With the Big Ten championship and Rose Bowl on the line." Great. A little late for those golden nuggets.

Our defense came up big, and we escaped with giving up just a field goal. Three points. That's the best Michigan could do. Given the potential for a disastrous touchdown, I was a little relieved. At 7-3, we still held the lead. But everyone, even the guys selling hotdogs, could sense that the feel of the game had changed. As I crossed the field and walked towards the southeast corner of the stadium towards our locker room, I was uncomfortably aware of a small chorus of boos. I'd heard a few boos in the stadium before, normally from the guys who wanted to speak to Earle in the only language their alcohol would allow. But this was different. This time they were booing me. And then there was the heckler in the South stands who verbally assaulted me as I made my way past him. A single Michigan alum in an OSU section—too old and well-dressed to be so drunk and obnoxious. Probably went to grad school there as well, I thought.

In the locker room, the halftime routine was normal but subdued. We knew Michigan shouldn't have been able to hang around at this point in the game. But there they were, just four points back. The assistant coaches went through our adjustments, and Earle gathered us for a final word of encouragement before heading back out to the field. There were a few "forget about its" thrown in my direction, but no panic or alarm. Obviously one can't literally forget about a boneheaded play, but neither should one dwell on its implications. I've never been a dweller. Oh sure, I was embarrassed that it had happened. But despite a reporter's later incredulity, it wasn't like I had to search the deep recesses of my soul to find the strength to carry on. This was football, not a movie on the Lifetime channel. All I wanted was another shot at a big play in the second half. One play that could shift the game's momentum—you cannot undo a bad decision. But there are two halves in football, each offering opportunities for success. And, I suppose, failure. But who thinks about failure in the middle of a Michigan game?

Michigan came out strong in the third quarter and dominated the statistics. With Byars slowed by his sore ankle and a Michigan defense that had adapted to our game plan, we struggled on offense. Meanwhile, their offense had finally found a rhythm and their sophomore quarterback started to look more poised. They held the ball for most of the quarter, and put another field goal on the board to make the score 7-6. Their usually accurate kicker missed another field goal a series later that would've given them the lead. We could sense, however, that they would eventually put more points on the board unless we started to pick up first downs.

The score was still 7-6 as the game moved into the fourth quarter. We finally got our tight end, Ed Taggart, involved in the offense and started to move the ball a little. But midway through the quarter, we found ourselves in yet another third-and-long situation on our own 43-yard line. If we didn't convert, one more punt could have given Michigan the ball and another chance at taking the lead. This deep into the game, one score could determine the final outcome.

As I lined up wide left for the third-and-12 play, I read the defensive secondary. They were in Cover 3, with the corners and safety playing thirds of the field. Tomczak called my number on an "in" route, which meant that I was supposed to run about 17 yards downfield before cutting to the inside across the field. Taggart lined up left and ran a straight clearing route down the center of the field. His job was to run the safety deep so I'd have room to come in behind him. As the ball was snapped I noticed that one of their linebackers decided to run with Taggart downfield. I knew immediately that this would cause a problem because the linebacker would clutter up the middle of the field, which was exactly where I wanted to go. Linebackers wouldn't normally drop so deep on this route, so when I started to make my break to the inside Tomczak and I both realized that we had to contend with an extra body to read.

As I came out of my break, I saw the linebacker to my right and a little in front of me. I had to decide whether to run through the route or to stop short of where he was positioned. I chose to run through the route, thinking I'd run past the congestion and hoping Tomczak would make the same read. He didn't. Instead he threw the ball where I would've been if I'd stopped short. I remember thinking momentarily that he and I would have to have one of those get-on-the-same-page quarterback-receiver chats after the play. Then I just reacted. The tough part was changing direction against my momentum. I knew I had to extend up and to the outside as far as I could go if I were to have a chance of getting a hand on the ball as it sailed past the linebacker's outstretched right arm. Luckily, I was able to jump far enough to get both hands up and make a solid grab at the ball. I came down and ensured I had possession before springing up and tossing the ball behind me. First down. Move the chains.

I'm not an expert on the subject, but I'd guess that part of creating a memorable moment is not realizing at the time you're creating a memorable moment. Ordinary often becomes remarkable, not by intent, but by circumstance and perception. The play would later be seen as pivotal in the outcome of the game. I've made better catches, but not on that stage and not in that moment and not in that context. Had we not scored on that possession, the catch would have been entirely forgettable, tucked away quietly into the big book of OSU football statistics as just another 17-yard reception. As it turned out, though, because I caught the ball we kept a drive alive and the momentum seemed to change. We scored a few plays later, and then again late in the quarter before running out the clock. We won the game 21-6, locking up the Big Ten championship and securing a berth in the 1985 Rose Bowl. As a result of the catch, I was named the Chevrolet Most Valuable Player of the game—of the Michigan game.

The Aftermath

To this day, to my constant amazement, total strangers approach me during Michigan week to congratulate me for the catch. No one ever seems to remember the fumble. Perhaps they're just being polite, but I suspect they've genuinely forgotten. If so, Emerson might be right, and we are all entitled to be remembered for our diving third-and-12 catches rather than our fumbled punts. I don't think it's that simple, but it'd be nice if life really worked that way. If they do remember the fumble, I'm curious as to why no one has ever asked me to explain my uneven performance that day.

My wife, who's not much of a football fan, thinks the whole thing is oddly amusing, especially the occasional autograph requests and ESPN Classics rebroadcasts. My kids think it's cool (for now). I'm not sure what to think anymore. When I was younger and cursed with an overactive introspection gland, I might have been tempted to explain that day with a profound and complex redemption theme that resulted from the metaphysical juxtaposition of success and failure. But I'm older now.

So, what then? How do I explain my performance? Could it be just what Earle, and Woody before him, taught all along? That football's about getting back up after you've been tackled—that it's not about success or failure, but both at the same time. And the question isn't whether either is permanent, but whether you choose to get up again, without fear or recrimination, after you've failed. *Ad infinitum.*

It's probably something like that. Although, if I asked them back then, I'm sure Earle and Woody would've found an even simpler and better explanation that somehow included an obsession with beating Michigan.

I'd love to hear that one.

***

Lanese, who with his wife, Laura, has a son, Michael, and daughters Camille and Francesca, said he was exposed to football at an early age. His father, Mike Lanese Jr., had played for legendary coach Ara Parseghian at Miami of Ohio. It was all sports, all the time for Lanese.

"It was a pretty normal suburban childhood," he said. "I was blessed with good coaches, starting with Coach Weisen at St. Francis CYO. In high school I played tailback for the Mayfield Wildcats under Coach Byron Morgan. During my senior year we were conference co-champs [Greater Cleveland Conference]."

How does Lanese want to be remembered as a Buckeye?

"... As the last receiver to wear high socks."

4

CHAMP HENSON

BIRTH DATE: June 1, 1953
HOMETOWN: Ashville, Ohio
RESIDENCE: Ashville, Ohio
POSITION: Fullback
HEIGHT: 6-foot-4
WEIGHT: 231 pounds
YEARS: 1972 to 1974

Fortified headgear proved to be the perfect battle gear for Harold "Champ" Henson, who would dive, head first, into a pile of humanity in an effort to gain a smidgen more yardage on a drive. The former OSU fullback is trying to acquire the same sort of protection for his son, Clayton, and his fellow U.S. Marines, who so often are the intended targets of roadside bombs in Iraq. Henson is part of Operation Helmet, a funding drive to provide free padded liners for Marines to protect them from brain injuries caused by blast concussion. ... Henson's 44 carries in a victory against Northwestern in the ninth game of the 1972 season set an Ohio State record that stands today. ... He was second-team All-Ohio and Back of the Year in the Central District as a high school senior at Teays Valley High School. Henson also played basketball and ran track in high school, "mostly so I wouldn't have to go home to farm." ... Henson had a brief stint for one season with the NFL's Cincinnati Bengals after his OSU days.

4

The Run-up

Paranoia apparently was boosted as Ohio State prepared to do battle with Michigan.

"It was usually the same with Coach [Woody Hayes], but notched up a bit during Michigan week," Champ Henson said. "We weren't allowed to talk to the media. During practice all week, they played crowd noise over the loudspeakers. Coach had managers looking for spies with binoculars at the Fawcett Center in case some spy had a room. We didn't know how much of this was for show or was for real. You never knew with Coach. He was such a great actor."

Game day presented itself with a backdrop that would make Grantland Rice smile.

"It was overcast and gloomy," Henson, then a sophomore, said. "It was the perfect day for football."

The Buckeyes fairly stuck to their routine for this game against The Team Up North, Henson said, although there were opportunities for a bit of extra motivation. For one, Michigan was the top-ranked team in the nation coming into Columbus, and Hayes "... had some senior players get up in front of us and tell us what the game meant to them. He had injured players, guys like Rick Seifert, I think, stand up and tell us how much he wished he could play against Michigan.

"While there was a lot of hype the week before the game, we were still disciplined and didn't deviate from our regular warmup or pregame routines. The locker room was pretty solemn; everyone was focusing on his tasks. We might have had a few more butterflies than normal; we were very excited and couldn't wait to get the game started. It was my first Michigan game, and I was ready to go."

Champ Henson takes the handoff from Cornelius Greene.

The Game

By Champ Henson

Michigan at Ohio State—November 25, 1972

It was loud. I'm sure the stadium was at capacity. Even during warmups, it seemed like it was packed early—more so than usual—and boisterous throughout the whole game.

This was the game of my life because in it we demonstrated such a great team effort. We had three goal-line defensive stands. Archie Griffin had a really good game. (Quarterback) Greg Hare played particularly well, especially when he ran the football.

Up until this game, the Michigan defense had never allowed their opponents to score more than five points. They were No. 1 in the country. They were such an awesome team, and there was so much back and forth between the two sides. They had a couple of chances to win it, too.

I was fortunate enough to score a touchdown. During the drive on which I scored, Greg Hare had made a really long run, and made it down to about the 5-yard line. I ran the off-tackle play, for which OSU was famous, and got down to the 1-yard line, and then ran the same play and plunged into the end zone. I have a picture of the touchdown that I scored, and you can't even see me. Everyone on both sides of the ball was in this picture in this pile. I remember I saw an opening between two offensive players' legs. I could see the goal line and zeroed in on that and somehow forced my way through.

During our sealing drive, I was watching Archie make a really great run of about 35 yards for a touchdown. I remember Michigan missing their field goal. Archie's touchdown seemed to turn the momentum.

Our three goal-line stands were unbelievable. After each defensive stand, we also seemed to gain some momentum. Standing there watching the defense play was just as exhausting. The defensive plays were really inspiring to the offense. We only scored 14 points, but that was more than any other team had scored against Michigan that year. It was an extremely hard-hitting game. Coach always told us that the Michigan game was the cleanest game of the year, and I believe that.

During that era, our two teams were very much alike. I remember being so tired during the game because, even when you weren't in the game, you were trying to sway the game with your thoughts—something like mental telepathy.

The Aftermath

Fans flooded the field after the monumental upset victory—one not many had given OSU a chance of getting. "I remember almost total exhaustion after the game," Henson said. "It was crazy. We were jubilant. Once we got into the locker room, we all just wanted to be together. There were guys crying. Coach had tears in his eyes, and his hair was messed up. John Hicks was crying and laughing at the same time.

"The defensive guys were physically and emotionally drained. The manager came in and told Coach that the President [Richard M. Nixon, one of Hayes' many political acquaintances] was on the phone. Coach told the manager to tell him, 'Hold on, I'm talking to the men.' He made the President wait on him. That's pretty impressive to a young kid. We felt important. It was such a great thing. We were all very close. This felt like the grand finale. However, we still had one more game, the Rose Bowl, but it was hard to regroup after this game."

(True enough. Ohio State went west and got pummeled by Southern Cal, 42-17, on New Year's Day.)

Still Henson and others savor the victory against the No. 1-ranked Wolverines all these years later. "While I had better efforts personally," he said, "This was my greatest accomplishment, because it was such a huge team effort. The camaraderie is what makes OSU football so special."

Henson was one of those "added starters" in the Ohio State recruiting machine.

"I grew up in a small town on a farm about 25 miles south of Columbus," he said. "Like any other kid growing up in Ohio, I wanted to play football. The irony was that Ohio State didn't really recruit me. I was going to go to Michigan to play for Bo [Schembechler, the Wolverines' legendary coach, who was Hayes' greatest rival on the field and closest friend away from football]. Two weeks before national signing day, Dick Walker, [Ohio State's] defensive-backfield coach came to see us. I was a little bit cold to him. I had already told Michigan I was going there. Coach Hayes and Coach Walker stopped by my house. A couple of days later, Coach Hayes came to my school. I saw him in the hall, and it reminded me of the Pied Piper with about 300 kids walking behind him. He was talking to them, having a great time.

"We went out and got a hamburger or something," Henson continued. "He took me home and drove around a bit and talked. I told him I wanted to come to Ohio State. My mom and dad asked him if he wanted to come in. He stayed on the porch; he told them he couldn't come in because he had been there twice already, and it would be a [recruiting rules] violation. I guess he knew the technicalities. He came to my basketball tournament. I think he wanted to get my picture in the paper and make it official."

No one could've predicted that Henson would be at Ohio State if his high school career was considered. "[I was] mediocre until my senior year at Teays Valley High School. Then I finally grew. I was always kind of a skinny guy, but then I started to put on weight. I also started to become kind of fast. A lot of schools wanted me to play defense, and with Ohio State, it was kind of a tossup, also.

"I didn't play very much defense my freshman year at Ohio State until they got us sorted out. In high school, I played defensive end, linebacker, and tailback. In my senior year, I scored 18 touchdowns and rushed for 1,300 yards in a nine-game season."

These days, you'll find Henson working a farm about five miles from the family plot he worked as a youth. He and his wife, Karen, who have four children, reside in Ashville. When he's not tending to the requirements of running a farming operation, Henson said he likes to do "typical outdoor types of activities: hunt, fish, work on the farm. I'm fortunate I get to make a living at something I enjoy."

He would like to be remembered as someone who did his part, or "a guy who played as hard as he could and contributed as much as he could to his team. I can't stress enough how close we were then and still are. They're such a great group of guys. I was fortunate to be a part of it all. I can't imagine my life without my time at Ohio State part of it."

5

JOE STAYSNIAK

BIRTH DATE: December 8, 1966
HOMETOWN: Elyria, Ohio
RESIDENCE: Brownsburg, Indiana
POSITION: Offensive tackle
HEIGHT: 6-foot-6
WEIGHT: 290 pounds
YEARS: 1986 to 1989

Staysniak was all-conference, all-county, and All-Ohio while at Midview High School, where he was inducted into its athletics hall of fame. He was voted the Lorain County Class AAA Defensive Lineman of the Year and was the Lorain County Lombardi Award winner. He was courted by many major colleges but answered to the call of Earle Bruce and the Ohio State Buckeyes. ... At Ohio State, his honors included All-Big Ten, GTF Academic All-America, the National Football Foundation, and the Hall of Fame Scholar-Athlete awards, as well as receiving the Big Ten Conference Medal of Honor and the Jack W. Stephenson Award (awarded by OSU College of Business for Athletic and Scholastic Achievement). He was also a team captain. ... He was drafted by the Buffalo Bills and played on their 1990 and 1991 AFC Championship teams. He retired from pro football in 1995 as a member of the 1995 AFC East Champion Indianapolis Colts.

The Run-up

The way Joe Staysniak recalls it, nobody outside of the Ohio State camp gave the Buckeyes much of a chance in the university's first, and only, appearance in the storied Cotton Bowl Classic at Dallas. "Very few people expected us to give Texas A&M a game, let alone win. The Aggies were well prepared, but it was our day."

Indeed. Ohio State won 28-12. "And it wasn't even that close," Staysniak said.

The Buckeyes had something for which to play. They wanted to send the seniors out as winners while proving all the doubters wrong.

Staysniak remembers the setting well: "It was a decent day. Dallas in January was much warmer than Columbus in January. OSU fans travel well, so we saw a lot of scarlet in the stadium. We also saw a lot of [Aggie] burgundy. So it was predominantly red—you just had to choose your shade."

The Buckeyes were in Dallas for a long run before kickoff.

"We spent the entire week there," Staysniak said. "They saw us as the team from up north. Texas A&M had been ranked very highly. The bowl committee treated us very well. However, the rest of the people we encountered weren't so nice, especially the girls. They were extremely arrogant.

"One night, when we were out at a bar, I heard some sorority girls—probably from SMU—making fun of the way we were dressed, because one of the guys had on Haggar slacks instead of a designer brand. We were a bunch of poor kids from Ohio who had no fashion sense. While it seemed like the fans looked at us like a bunch of Yankees, the [Texas A&M] players appeared to respect us."

Adding insult to previous insults was an oral dustup between Bruce and a motorcycle police officer, who was to be providing a clear path to the Cotton Bowl for the Ohio State buses.

"Usually, we had a police escort from the hotel to the game to ensure that we arrived on time in traffic," Staysniak explained. "During our trip, the motorcycle cops escorting us stopped at every light, thereby eliminating the need for an escort. At the third stop,

Joe Staysniak says the team was never "so focused."

Earle got off the bus. He walked over to one of the cops and got his finger in his face and just started ripping him, like he used to do to us. We couldn't hear what he was saying, but we could see his lips moving. The cops took off and left us. We felt like a little kid, when you see your dad angry. The bus driver drove us unescorted.

"First the girls, then the cops. This set the tone for our game. It was a pride thing—us against all of them. I'd never seen our team so focused."

The Game

By Joe Staysniak

Ohio State vs. Texas A&M
The Cotton Bowl—January 1, 1987

Playing in this game was like putting a big bow on what it's like to play for Ohio State. We were being disrespected in a game of that magnitude. Everyone hated us. Everyone wanted a piece of us. Millions of people were watching. We knew we had to live up to the tradition and put our best foot forward. I remember thinking that the armed forces would be listening to the game on the radio. We were aware of things like that.

While we were out of our comfort zone in Texas, we knew that fans everywhere were cheering us on. It was a blast. Everything was tied up into this one game. This was something the entire country focused on. With the OSU-Michigan game, the audience is more limited to those two schools and states. This game put us on the map in the south. It helped start a tradition of Ohio State taking on top teams in new locations.

I was a fresh-faced, red-shirt freshman, and A&M's defensive tackle was a senior ... with a mustache. I felt like a young kid going against a 40-year-old man. I couldn't grow any facial hair—then or now. Yet, I still held my own.

It was great to come back to the huddle and look each other in the eye, and say, "Yup, I'm doing my job." It was a job we loved and were focused on. It wasn't a perfect game, but we weathered every storm. We didn't make any huge mistakes.

I remember getting a cowboy hat and a watch. The watch worked for two weeks. I still have it, though, because it has the Cotton Bowl (emblazoned) on it. I was excited to have the cowboy hat, although I didn't know where I would be able to wear it. Then I got some cowboy boots, so I thought I was going to wear my Cotton Bowl cowboy hat to my girlfriend's home in Houston. But the hat and shoes were different colors.

I remember after the game, one of the bowl committee guys, who was definitely a Texan, came in afterwards and was polite and gracious. The bowl committee treated us well. Everything about the bowl was a class act.

The Aftermath

While ultimately the greatest game of his career at OSU, Staysniak said, he didn't catch on to its importance immediately.

"Being young and inexperienced, it didn't hit me like it did those seniors who were playing their last game," he said. "I was very happy. We had won, and I enjoyed the closeness of playing with my team. I remember looking around at the seniors who we were able to send off with a win. When you come back to campus for things like homecoming, warm feelings are generated when you think of games like this. My junior and senior years were different. I didn't have a lot of great memories. However, with our success in games like the Cotton Bowl, I'm able to look back and be happy about the whole experience. I was part of the 'good old days,' part of the Woody [Hayes-] like tradition with Earle."

Of what is he most proud regarding his days at Ohio State?

"It's hard to pick one thing. I'm proud of graduating *cum laude*; I'm proud of being part of a great team; I'm proud of being a co-captain; and I'm proud of my involvement with the 'Earle' headbands during the Michigan game [five days after Bruce was terminated by the university, he still coached his last regular-season game in 1987, and the team wore the Earle headbands in support of their coach]. Being part of that tradition is something that you take with you to the next level.

"When I played in the pros, we always had side bets on the OSU games. I've carried the Ohio State traditions with me everywhere, in the pros and in life. Football, while being entertainment, was a great vehicle for me to get my education—and to honor my mom, who was a teacher, and my dad, who was a police officer."

Staysniak said he ultimately settled at OSU for a variety of reasons.

"While I was being recruited, it was nice to say that I was being recruited by Ohio State," he said, unapologetically. "There was instant credibility and respect when Ohio State was mentioned. My ultimate goal was to get a scholarship so that my mom and dad did not have to pay for school. It was prestigious to play for Ohio State. I grew up watching games every week, and watching all of the greats—[Art] Schlichter, [Cornelius] Greene, [Jack] Tatum. To be a part of that tradition was amazing. Plus, being close to home, my dad could work around his police duties and come to the games—as could my aunts and uncles. I was able to start for four years. It was great to be in the right place at the right time. I was grateful that Earle saw something in me."

Growing up in Grafton, Ohio, gave this lad a chance to dream of the Big Time.

"I was recruited by Stanford to play defense," Staysniak said. "We were a farm school and never won a championship. My senior year we were pretty good, but lost to our archrival on an extra-point kick that I missed. A high school classmate, Kelly McCartney, recruited me to go to Colorado. Kelly was the niece of Colorado coach and founder of Promise Keepers, Bill McCartney.

"While in high school, I never wanted to come off the field. I was an offensive tackle, a defensive tackle, and a kicker. Because I was a kicker I had to come off the field for at least one play to change shoes. I was taught well at an early age to hustle and get my can down the field all the time. I was taught to do the little things like pick up my teammates on the field. I remember [center] Kirk Lowdermilk had the same attitude about hard work on the field. I took what I learned from my high school coaches to Ohio State, and then I took what I learned at Ohio State to the pros."

In addition to football, Staysniak also played basketball at Midview ("I sat the bench"), ran track, and played baseball ("I tried to work on my hand-eye coordination").

These days, work finds him behind the microphone for WIBC (1070-AM) in Indianapolis. It's a job he began while playing for the Indianapolis Colts. "They asked me to do a recap once a week during morning drive. I also filled in during the year on the evening sports-talk show. Now, I do sports during afternoon drive. We cover the Colts, Pacers, Fever, and all the races at the Indianapolis Motor Speedway."

He met his future bride, Pam, in spring quarter of his senior year at Ohio State. They celebrated their 14th anniversary in June 2006. The couple has two young sons, with whom he enjoys "... anything outdoors ... we live on 20 acres and enjoy fishing, cycling, swimming, and woodworking."

Staysniak wants to be remembered "... as someone who gave my all every time I stepped on the field or in the classroom. I started for four years and never took a play off. It is still an honor to be part of the greatest tradition in college football. I gave 100 percent to the university both on and off the field, but have gotten it back in spades. The whole process worked great for me, and I hope the university feels the same way."

6

JOHN HICKS

BIRTH DATE: March 21, 1951
HOMETOWN: Cleveland, Ohio
RESIDENCE: Columbus, Ohio
POSITION: Offensive tackle
HEIGHT: 6-foot-4
WEIGHT: 255 pounds
YEARS: 1970 to 1972

A former All-Ohio lineman at Cleveland John Hay High School. ... A three-year letterman at OSU, an All-Big Ten and All-America selection and winner of the Lombardi Award and the Outland Trophy following the 1972 season. ... Enshrined in the College Football Hall of Fame in 2001. ... Played professionally with the New York Giants and the Pittsburgh Steelers.

The Run-up

John Hicks simply had grown tired of being cannon fodder for the varsity during the 1969 season. When his sophomore year dawned, he was fully prepared to take advantage of any opening to become a starter—and that he did.

With the horribly bitter taste lingering from the previous season's 24-12 undoing of the then-No.1-rated Buckeyes at Michigan—a perfect season spoiled—Hicks and his teammates set their sights on the rematch as soon as the final gun sounded. The underclassmen told themselves they would make a difference.

"My freshman year, we sat home and listened to the loss to Michigan," said Hicks. "It was a huge shock. As freshmen, we didn't think anyone—and I mean *anyone*—could beat our varsity. We practiced against them day after day. I mean, Kern, Tatum, Brockington ... they were all household names. When we lost up there, that's when I really understood what it meant to be a Buckeye. They took away our honor."

And so the vanquished returned from Ann Arbor led by a rotund man wearing a black-wool baseball cap who all but declared war. Woody Hayes never referred to his Big Ten Conference opponent specifically, but every time he mentioned "... that school up north," everyone knew to which school he was referring.

"Revenge isn't a strong enough word," Hicks said of Hayes' motives in preparing for the Wolverines the next fall. "As soon as they got back to town, we started preparing. All the winter-quarter [conditioning] workouts were more intense—*way more*. All 25 practices in the spring were about Michigan. He was—and I guess we were, too—obsessed with paying them back. We even had that carpet with 'Michigan' on it outside the locker room. We walked across 'them' each day and in the game, too. And I kind of had an advantage there, because I was quick enough to handle their slant tackles on defense. The year before, they manhandled us. I worked and worked that spring, determined not to let that happen again. It was my first

This game, John Hicks says, was about honor.

shot. I wanted to make sure they remembered me. From Day One of spring ball, I started working on the slant tackle, and I never let up."

"Michigan had enough of me after three years," Hicks smiled. "I would cut them off, and then block and block and block. That's why I started, because I could block Michigan's slant tackle."

It didn't hurt that Hicks was a highly accomplished right-side protector and agile enough to lead ball carriers down the field. Hayes called Hicks the greatest lineman he ever coached. In this game, as a fresh-faced sophomore, he might very well have planted the seeds for what ultimately would become Hayes' proclamation.

Game day dawned bright, sunny, and a bit crisp, although perhaps warmer than would be expected of a late-November Saturday. Hicks recalls nothing out of the ordinary happening that morning, mostly just the routine of rise and shine, grabbing breakfast, attending the position meeting, and then checking out of the hotel for the bus ride to Ohio Stadium. "We were taken out of the dorms on Wednesday. It was crazy. They wanted us focused, which was easy to see why."

The coaches wondered about John Hicks when the team arrived at the stadium. "I wasn't all hyped up or anything like that, but they were worried about me. I, personally, never worried about anything with the game. ... I graded out at 97 percent, and the Old Man said that I had what it took. There was some talk in the locker room about this and that, but I just kind of kept quiet. Then, before we went out onto the field, there was some commotion with telegrams arriving from members of the '64 and '69 teams, wishing us luck and hoping we'd kick their butts. Then Coach Hayes was kind of 'moved,' if you know what I mean—then the room got real quiet. When we finally left that locker room and stepped onto the field, everybody just went nuts!"

The Game

By John Hicks

Michigan at Ohio State—November 22, 1970

On the field, we wouldn't even look at them. We were well aware that they had knocked us out of our 22-game winning streak and out of the Rose Bowl the year before. There was a lot of animosity on our side. There was so much at stake with the Rose Bowl and national championship implications. We were both undefeated and untied. Back then, it was one-and-done—lose and stay home. We weren't about to lose.

When we went back into the locker room right before kickoff, everybody went nuts again. It was just unbelievable. I can't explain it. At that point, you see, the coaches are out of it; the players just take over, and either you're ready or you're not. We were.

We wanted it more than Michigan ... for nearly a whole year. That was the biggest game of my life. I just knew it would be special, and I really thought I would have a special day. After all the work we put in, how could we miss?

I remember, at kickoff, Michigan fumbled on our side of the 50-yard line. It was pretty quiet in the huddle. I was just listening to Rex (Kern). Everything was under control. I had this confidence that it was about to be a great game for us.

We were winning 10-3 by the half, and ultimately, we won 20-9. But we were going full-bore, even on that last drive. You never could turn your back on them.

When we were walking back into the locker room after the game, that's when it began to sink in ... what I accomplished ... what we accomplished. And the really great thing is all we did was follow the plan and execute it. It wasn't until we looked at the film of that game that I realized really what I had done and what we had done. We beat 'em up pretty good. Actually, we manhandled them.

I gave every ounce of everything I had that day. I wouldn't do anything differently if I had the chance to do it all over again.

The Aftermath

In the wake of "the biggest game of my life," Hicks remembers feeling accomplished as a 19-year-old. "My parents, Charity and John, were going nuts, because of the Rose Bowl [berth] and everything, and I remember just sitting with Tate [Jack Tatum] and the guys and letting it all soak in."

Hicks would return for his junior and senior seasons, replicating his expertise at his position for each campaign. There was no other way. "I knew how to play one way: prepared," he said. "So did everybody else on that team, and that's why we were so good."

Hicks said he remembers, as a senior, telling Archie Griffin that the offensive line would do its part to get him 1,500 yards. "He would say, 'Stop saying that!' Archie was, and is, so humble. He is an outstanding person with high morals. But anyway, we got him 1,583 yards his sophomore year, and we teased him about the '... need to remember the little guys who made it possible.' I kept my word. I protected him like I would a little brother."

The road to Ohio State was decorated with fond childhood memories for Hicks.

"We were a close family," said Hicks, the eldest of three siblings, "and there was always something fun going on in the house. My parents worked hard and provided for us, my dad as a mechanic for the state, and my mom was a nurse. We were a middle-class family with no hardships, no peril; my parents saw to that. There was a lot of love, and we're still passing it around."

The young John Hicks spent his non-school hours "... playing ball a lot, and hanging out around the Cleveland Browns. I got to know them really well, guys like Bob Brown, the offensive lineman, who went on to the [Oakland] Raiders. It was cool to hang out with them. Guys like [Hall of Fame inductees] Jim Brown and Paul Warfield lived in the neighborhood. They were all my friends and role models, and it remains that way today."

Today, Hicks is the proud papa of Alyssa, a marketing executive; Alayna, an accountant; Amarah, a vice president in the Veterans

Administration; and Brandon, an attorney. He and his wife, Cindy, live in Columbus, where he is a partner in Covington Realty Advisors.

When Hicks isn't working or spending time with his extended family, which includes his fellow OSU alums, he is either on the golf course, fishing for bass, or "play-fighting" with his dear friends, Tatum and Phil Strickland, who have become his children's "evil uncles."

"It's disgusting!" Hicks protested. "They have ruined my kids—spoiled them rotten. My kids tell *them* everything. Me? Nothing!"

Asked how he would like to be remembered as a Buckeye, Hicks, as is his custom, didn't hesitate: "A good teammate—just leave it at that."

7

BRUCE ELIA

BIRTH DATE: January 10, 1953
HOMETOWN: Cliffside Park, New Jersey
RESIDENCE: Cliffside Park, New Jersey
POSITIONS: Fullback/linebacker
HEIGHT: 6-foot-1
WEIGHT: 217 pounds
YEARS: 1972 to 1974

"During my senior year at OSU, I was drafted in the NFL by the Miami Dolphins in the fourth round as a linebacker," Elia said. *"I played in Miami for one year, and then I was traded to the San Francisco 49ers and played four more years before retiring. Our senior year, 17 players were drafted into the NFL." ... Elia was all-league and all-county in football, basketball, and track and field in high school. In track, he threw the discus and shot put, and he was ranked in the top five in New Jersey in discus. He also was a third-team All-State basketball player. "My basketball team beat a team that was the defending state champion with a 44-0 record. They also totally outsized us,"* he said. *"Our town honored us for this championship, and we received recognition from the state legislature. I'm still close with a lot of those guys on my basketball team. ... It was great to come back to Jersey and be surrounded by my friends and family."*

The Run-up

It began three months earlier. Coach Woody Hayes had Ohio State practicing for this game in the August heat, said Bruce Elia, a fullback-turned-linebacker. In stark contrast to the soaring temperatures and humidity of late summer was a frigid, sunless day greeting the players on the morning of Elia's game of his life.

Still, the bundled-up partisans in Ohio Stadium had no problem getting up—or staying warm—for the big one. Elia said: "It was electric, magic. It was like a security blanket. When you're home in the Horseshoe, and everyone was in scarlet and gray, it's a powerful feeling. On this day, we were playing for the Big Ten Championship and a trip to the Rose Bowl and a possible rematch with USC for a national title. Everyone in the country knew this was the day, and this was the game. And remember, this was Michigan, our archrival."

With those August practices still fresh in their minds, the Old Man put the Buckeyes through a hellacious practice just two days before the game.

"Our Thursday practice was our final tough, physical practice that week; and we were pumped," Elia recalls. "The Thursday night before the Michigan game, a bunch of us guys—me, Steve Meyers, our All-America center, [defensive back] Steve Luke, and some other defensive players got together to play cards until midnight to take the tension off the upcoming big game. Woody had put up the traveling squad in a local hotel that night, which was unusual."

Friday dawned, and the focus sharpened. "Everything became serious," Elia continued. "Our Friday practice was all about preventing mental errors. The physical preparation was done Monday to Thursday. The mood changed dramatically from Thursday to Friday. We were serious and didn't feel like laughing. It was like we were preparing for war, especially on defense because we had to stop the powerful Michigan offense. On Saturday, we'd wake up; eat a little by eight, but not too much because of our nerves. Woody used to tell us, 'First to eat, last to fight.'"

Bruce Elia, who did time at fullback, was credited with 19 tackles in the Michigan game.

Finally getting to game day actually brought the team a bit of relief—the realization that the hard work was behind them. All they had to do was go out and execute what they had been taught.

"It was a great feeling to know that the day had finally arrived," Elia said. "The bus ride [to the stadium] was quiet. You could hear a pin drop. In the locker room, everyone was getting taped and padded. We all knew the game was going to be extremely physical. This was what we'd been preparing for since our arrival on campus. This was the pinnacle. The whole country was watching. Our parents, families, friends would be watching us. 'The Star Spangled Banner' took forever to sing before the kickoff!"

Preparations weren't quite complete. Hayes took one last opportunity to weigh in on what was at stake.

"Just before kickoff, Woody reminded us what was on the line," Elia said. " We all knew. He said we had to do the basics, which were block, tackle, and run hard with the ball. He said, 'We don't need one [defensive] guy hitting the ball carrier, we need three.' He told Archie [Griffin, the eventual two-time Heisman Trophy-winning tailback] he had to have his best game. Then Woody launched into one of his wartime stories that would raise us to the roof. He made us feel we were fighting for America, and we were the good guys. Michigan was the national enemy. The next three hours would be a blank for me. I was in the 'zone,' and I couldn't get out of it."

The Game

By Bruce Elia

Michigan at Ohio State—November 23, 1974

Once we began playing, we calmed down because it usually felt good to start hitting someone and get physical. First of all, it was the Michigan game of my senior year and the last game of the regular season. If we lost, we did not go anywhere. In those days, the Rose

Bowl was the only bowl game a Big Ten team could play in. There weren't any other bowl games like today.

We were ranked second or third in the country after having been the No. 1 team for seven weeks. We had been playing together for four years. For me, this was possibly my best game ever.

Michigan scored 10 points in the first quarter, and we were down, 10-0. Going into the second quarter, I made an interception in Michigan territory, which led to a field goal to make it 10-3. We kicked another field goal, and it was 10-6, and then a third field goal to make it 10-9. It was a very hard-fought, physical game—just what we expected. We were well-prepared, though. In the fourth quarter, we took the lead on our fourth field goal of the day. We were finally leading, 12-10.

I was in on 19 tackles and was being more active than I'd ever been. I was playing my heart out with guys that I loved and against my biggest enemy. The score kept going back and forth. Everyone started stepping up to the plate, making big plays. It was 12-10 and late in the fourth quarter. It came down to the wire. Michigan had the ball and was driving on us. As Michigan was moving toward scoring position, defensive lineman Pete Cusick got a sack. And then I had a tackle for a loss. Michigan lined up to kick a field goal with 16 seconds on the clock—a 32-yard field goal. After the ball was snapped and kicked, I remember looking back at the goal posts seeing the ball fade to the side. It was really close.

Immediately, thousands of fans rushed the field. I had two high school friends from New Jersey jump on me while I was on the field. It seemed like the entire crowd was on the field. They had to clear the place for the next couple of plays.

But, of course, we knew it was over. We had defeated the enemy. America was a safe place once again, and we were going to the Rose Bowl to play USC.

The Aftermath

In the wake of a rollercoaster, brutally physical game, emotions swirled around the OSU locker room.

"We were exhausted, sweating, hurt, happy, exhilarated, and surrounded by our family and best friends," Elia said warmly. "Woody came in and gave us a great congratulatory speech. We had the best feeling of accomplishment. Not too often in life do you work so long and so hard for one thing on the line. It was such a tremendous relief because we'd been thinking about this game for seven to eight months since our spring practice. No other [matchup] in the country—well, maybe two or three others—can compare. You come out of this tremendous competition surrounded by tradition with such a sense of accomplishment. And the best part is that you've accomplished it with your best friends, the guys you've been bonded with for years. The guys you've practiced with and banged up against for four years.

"Yes, that was the top for me because it was The Big Game. I had also had one of my best games, and it was that much better, because there was so much on the line. And, my parents, brothers, sister, and girlfriend were there—and, of course, it was on national TV."

Elia said he selected Ohio State more for what it wasn't than for what it was. "Going to OSU was the best decision of my life. had been recruited by approximately 75 schools. I visited Penn State because I liked Joe Paterno and the Nittany Lions. During my visit, the guys took me out on a Saturday night to a Pizza Hut in the middle of the woods.

"You have to remember, I had been a kid growing up in New Jersey, hanging out on street corners until late in the evening. I came from a hard-working construction family. We worked hard during the week, but then we needed to have fun on the weekends. Penn State wasn't for me. Pizza only on Saturday night wasn't enough fun for me.

"Next I visited Notre Dame," Elia continued. "They had a ballplayer who took me around campus on a Saturday night, and we stopped at a fraternity house. I was thinking, 'Here's the big night.' He took me out for Kentucky Fried Chicken, and then at 10 p.m. said it was time to go home and study. I canned Notre Dame."

A subsequent trip brought Elia to Columbus. On arrival, he met Assistant Coach Glen Mason (now the head coach at Minnesota), a New Jersey native—a natural bond, as one might suspect.

"He said, 'I got you a date,' and he took me out with his girlfriend—who I think became his wife—and her friend. While we were out, he took me to High Street. It looked like 42d Street in New York City. I saw thousands of kids everywhere. We were down by (noted hangout) Papa Joe's, and he told me how [campus] was laid out. He said that on the left is the school, and 'That's where we go to class and study.' He said on the right are the fraternity and sorority houses and off-campus housing. But down the middle, he said, 'That's where we party.' He told me that High Street had 17 bars in a one-mile distance, and few people could make it to the end and have a drink in each bar. So, it was pretty clear to me. While all the other schools were as solid academically as OSU, no one else had High Street. After that weekend, I knew I wanted to become a Buckeye."

Shortly after his return home, Elia's father—"a hard-working, strong man"—asked his son if he liked Ohio State enough to commit to attending on a scholarship.

"I told him I was a bit intimidated by the powerhouse that Ohio State represented," Elia said. "They had guys like Rex Kern, Jack Tatum, John Brockington, and Jim Stillwagon. These guys were made of steel. He told me, 'If you're going to play, play with the best.' He gave me a challenge, and I took it. It was the best decision of my life."

Elia's upbringing, of course, involved a fair amount of sports. "In high school, I played running back and linebacker, just as I did at Ohio State. I had a very good sophomore and junior year, and I got a chance to play some of the top players in the county and northern New Jersey. My senior year, I had a tough time because I weighed 195 pounds, and my linemen weighed 150 pounds. I was the big target in the backfield. It was a punishing year, but I tried to play well. I still received a lot of athletic honors. That year made me tougher."

Elia today is the owner of a Prudential Real Estate franchise "about 10 minutes from where I grew up. And I still get together to play basketball with the guys I grew up with."

He has four children—three daughters and one son. "My son is a sophomore and second-string quarterback at the University of New Hampshire," Elia said. "I have two daughters at Ohio State. One is in veterinary school, and the other is a freshman. I took them to OSU games when they were growing up. They all loved it. Their mom, Lori, also went to Ohio State. We are a Buckeye family living in New Jersey."

While Elia keeps his basketball game going, he still has time for new endeavors. "Skiing is my newest hobby. I love to go skiing with my family. I also play golf and Ping Pong, and I go biking and trapshooting."

In considering his Buckeye legacy, Elia declared: "I got hurt on my second day at OSU. I was out for a month. From then on, it always felt like an uphill battle. I was always working extra hard to get caught up. My worst injury became my biggest asset. Too many guys started out strong and then faded. I always had to work extra hard. I was afraid to go back to where I was when I was injured—not playing. I made sure I put in extra time for fear someone would take my job. Plus, I enjoyed the personal challenge. I hope to be remembered as part of a great group of guys, and as a team player who always gave 110 percent and beat the odds."

8

ARNIE CHONKO

BIRTH DATE: May 17, 1943
HOMETOWN: Parma, Ohio
RESIDENCE: Overland Park, Kansas
POSITION: Safety
HEIGHT: 6-foot-2
WEIGHT: 204 pounds
YEARS: 1962 to 1964

Chonko played for Parma (Ohio) High School, where his coach was Bob Brugge. "I played both ways, and was the quarterback on offense. I was All-State, All-Ohio, and a lot of those other things," he said, modestly. Chonko also played baseball and basketball in high school. "I was also All-America in baseball at Ohio State," he said. "In fact, I was a trivia question in one of the programs as to being All-America in both baseball and football. Baseball was my better sport." Dr. Chonko was drafted by both the Detroit Lions and the Miami Dolphins of the NFL as well as the Cleveland Indians and the Detroit Tigers. However, he turned down these opportunities to attend medical school at Ohio State.

The Run-up

It was that week's clash of the titans. Two undefeated teams locking horns on a bright, sunny Midwestern day, or, as Arnie Chonko puts it, "The most beautiful autumn day you could have imagined."

A conspicuous buzz radiated through the crowd, with each team coming in undefeated, "It always amazed me that with 80-90,000 fans there every week that we could hear ourselves," he said. "We could hear each other on the field because the noise traveled upwards.

"I loved the band. My junior or senior year was the year that they came up with 'Hang on Sloopy.' I remember telling Jim Nein in the huddle, 'Hey, that's a catchy tune.' And it has stood the test of time, to be sure.

"Woody [Hayes] sequestered us in a hotel, the Stouffer Inn on Olentangy River Road, I think," Chonko said. "Our ritual was to get up in the morning and get taped at the hotel. Our coaches took us in groups for a walk around the neighborhood to get us stretched out before we ate. People were out. My girlfriend [now my wife] saw us taking our walk. I couldn't say anything. I could only wave at her.

Before the game against Southern Cal, Chonko said, he had spent a lot of time that week "studying their films and the tendency sheets. I kept my eye on their running back, Mike Garrett, because I was the defensive back and safety on the wide side. Garrett was short and quick. He eventually played for the Kansas City Chiefs and became USC's athletic director.

"I remember getting nervous before games and getting butterflies in my stomach. Some guys would actually throw up. One of Woody's classic moves before a big game was to stand out by the door with only the starters remaining inside. As we filed out of the locker room, he would make all of us promise him that we would play the greatest game of our lives. We had to repeat, 'I'm going to play the greatest game of my life …' and shake his hand."

The Game

By Arnie Chonko

Southern California at Ohio State—October 17, 1964

Both teams went into the game undefeated. We had put in some man-to-man defense successfully against Illinois and wanted to do the same against USC. Our defensive coaches, Frank Elwood and Max Uhrick, had to sneak in the man-to-man coverage without telling Woody. One of them said, "Don't blow it, boys, because I don't want to die." USC had so much talent and speed that I knew we could not cover them playing straight-zone defense.

I'm 6-foot-2, and because Garrett was short, I thought I'd have him, and when he'd cut sharply, I'd grab him by any means possible— shoulder pad, belt, whatever—until the rest of my troops arrived. He never fumbled. On one play, I saw a screen pass coming. I felt awfully alone out there with him. I forced him to the inside—he probably ran 12 yards—until Ike Kelly arrived. We were able to keep him from breaking out.

During the second quarter, after we scored at the end of a long drive to make it 7-0, Southern Cal got the ball down to our 30-yard line.

We pressured the quarterback and were able to sack him. They had a tendency to throw down-and-out passes or go deep up the sidelines for the score. They ran that play, and I did not bite. I was prepared to run deep with him, and I was able to tip it away.

I'd noticed on the game films that USC had the tendency to curl the wide receiver and send Garrett out of the backfield on a circle route. I thought they might be doing that next. Sure enough, they did. We sent in a blitz. USC quarterback Craig Furtig tried to throw, but I intercepted on about the 25-yard line with visions of glory. The end zone flashed before my eyes. I started running up the left sideline, but

Arnie Chonko made a key deflection in his greatest game as a Buckeye.

USC was coming on me. I cut back. Next thing I knew, I was on about the 30- to 50-yard line, and I felt like I'd been hit by a truck. I went flying through the air. We were never allowed to go on the field without our mouth guards, but I hated wearing mine, so I stuck it in my jock. I had been running and had my mouth open when I got hit, shattering my molars. I had white pieces of my tooth in my hand as I was walking off the field.

The locker room was tense at halftime as we were clinging to a 7-0 lead.

USC came out of locker room after the half in a "tackle eligible" formation, which had worked against us previously. This time, however, we picked it up ... our defensive end crushed the guy.

Ike Kelley, a linebacker who was also the deep snapper, was the center, and I would hold the ball during the snap. I told it him not to snap it high, but that if he had to snap it low, I could get it. ... He told me, "Thanks for the confidence." Before every kick, I told our kicker, Bob Funk, that it was a piece of cake. And next it was 10-0.

We coughed up the ball, and USC appeared to be in business on our side of the 50-yard line. They got down to our 9-yard line, I think. It was goal-to-go. They spread us all over the field. I was spread out on their wide receiver. I knew they loved to throw a quick slant on first down, so I lined up on the outside. I knew I could get on the inside to get him on the slant. I blocked the wide receiver, and the quarterback couldn't get the pass off and was sacked.

So now it was second down. I tried to figure out what their next move would be. The films showed they would possibly try to run it again, but they flanked out again. I lined up with the wide receiver, who faked a slant and tried to cut the corner. I tried to run with him, and as he cut out to the corner of the flag, I saw his eyes go up, I knew I better be looking for the ball. I looked back and saw the ball coming and dived for it. It made a great picture and was in *The Columbus Dispatch* the next day. Unfortunately, the ball ricocheted off my fingers. It would have been the best interception of my career, but at least I broke up the play.

Third down dawned, and USC again went to the inside slant. I ran the curl pattern to Garrett, who came in the circle route. I had my eyes on him. Next thing I knew, a red blur hit him and knocked him flat ... out of bounds.

Everyone knows that you get in the pile or you stay away from the pile. I stupidly went within yards of the pile. One of their offensive linemen knocked me head over heels, and I rolled unceremoniously onto the track. Clearly it was a (personal) foul, but it wasn't called. I remember calling him an SOB, but he just laughed. I swore a blood oath. The line judge yelled at me to calm down. I was really ticked and embarrassed. USC was noteworthy as cheap-shot artists. I remember his number was 64, but I don't remember his name. I went back to the huddle and told them that, if anyone got a chance, they should take a shot at No. 64. I tried to get him the rest of the game.

On the fourth down of that series, I was still shaking. I lost my focus. Fortunately, they went to the other side of the field, throwing to Don Harkins. We got the ball on about our 38-yard line, sparking another change in momentum.

With little time remaining, USC started passing, but we were able to continue the pressure. One of their guys caught a down-and-out pass, but was tackled. I came up to the pile around midfield. I got knocked head over heels again into the Southern Cal bench—and again, they did not call a penalty. The Southern Cal bench was laughing at me. I remember getting up with Coach (John) McKay not too far away. I said to one of the USC guys, "Before you laugh at me, best you get on the field, surfer boy. I'm playing and you're sitting."

Coach McKay, who was a lot different than Woody said, "That's a pretty good line."

The Aftermath

According to Chonko, nothing is finer than winding down the clock with the comfort that you own the game's outcome.

"You kneel with your teammates and talk about how you did it," he said. "In football, you're so dependent on each other. When you come off the field [with a win], the Victory Bell rings in the southeast tower. You could hear it ringing off the field. Writers came up to us with pencil and paper—no cameras, no tape recorders. We didn't have press conferences in those days. I celebrated with my family and girlfriend and went out to dinner.

"Typically, I'd rehash the game, play by play, with my two older brothers. I didn't party because I was more of a serious student," Chonko explained. "I liked school and liked the opportunity to get an education that Ohio State provided me. My parents were both very bright, but weren't able to have much of a formal education because of the Depression."

The bottom line on Chonko's game of his life?

"Coach Hayes was effusive in his praise for the defense," he said. "I think he gave the game ball to all the defensive players. He said, 'You guys can share it,' and he had us all on his Sunday morning television show."

Chonko said as great as the victory over USC was, he takes a huge measure of pride in "... being able to be a good teammate and being able to cover for guys, especially as a safety—being a coach on the field [and] making sure things were done right."

Ultimately an All-American at Ohio State, Chonko said, "I was thrilled to play and represent the university. I was truly a student-athlete. I went to school to learn and get an education. It's impossible to grow up in Ohio playing football and not consider going to school at OSU. The only two schools I considered were Ohio State and Notre Dame. I listened to both teams on the radio. When you're in high school, and Coach Hayes shows up and says, 'We want you,' it's hard to resist. Besides, Ohio State had everything I wanted in a school—a great football team and an excellent medical school. Woody Hayes was a master recruiter. He took me over to the medical school and had the dean take me to lunch. I was just a kid. The dean told me if I got a 3.5 [grade-point average], or even a 3.2 since I was playing football, and did well in the sciences, then I could get into med school there.

"Woody sold the whole tradition. He told us that we owed it to our state to go to OSU. He knew the whole tradition thing would work with a recruit. It worked with me. After I got there and started playing as a sophomore; it was like, 'Pinch me—this can't be real!'"

* * *

These days, he is Dr. Arnold Chonko, a professor of nephrology at University of Kansas School of Medicine. "I really enjoy teaching med students, especially in things like history," he said.

He and his wife, Barbara, have been married 40 years.

"We were childhood sweethearts," he said. "She went to Miami of Ohio. She's been a master teacher for 17 years and teaches third grade. We have four children. My oldest son is in business in San Mateo. My youngest played OSU baseball and has a Master's degree and teaches math and coaches. My oldest daughter has her MBA and works in marketing in Chicago; and my youngest daughter works as an elementary school teacher in Kansas City."

In his off hours, Chonko said he studies history—"I love history"—and watches the History Channel. "My wife is a musician, and I enjoy jazz and big bands. I also golf once a week with my son," he said.

Chonko would prefer OSU fans to remember him and his team not merely for one game, but "… as someone who gave my best to the university in athletics; as someone who was very reliable and did not make many mistakes and who helped my teammates with some of the mental aspects of the game; and as a kid coming out of [suburban] Cleveland who was thrilled to play there. I got more out of the university than I deserved, including med school."

Or, he said, you may choose to remember him as "Old Reliable."

9

BOB HOYING

BIRTH DATE: September 20, 1972
HOMETOWN: St. Henry, Ohio
RESIDENCE: Dublin, Ohio
POSITION: Quarterback
HEIGHT: 6-foot-4
WEIGHT: 224 pounds
YEARS: 1992 to 1995

He was All-State as a junior and senior at St. Henry High School, and all-county, too. "We also won the basketball state championship my junior and senior years and won the football state championship my senior year. I think one other team might have won both the state basketball and state football championships in the same year," Hoying said. ..."I ran track, the 110 high hurdles, high jump, long jump, and 4x100 relay. At a school like St. Henry, you had to play all sports for us to field teams. ... As a kid of about eight or nine, the first player I remember watching at Ohio State was Art Schlichter," Hoying said. "I remember sitting down with my dad, watching him play. He wrote me a three-page letter about how happy he was for me to be breaking his records my senior year. I think it was the single-season passing yardage record, or it might have been touchdowns; I broke them both about the same time. To get a letter from him—even though it wasn't during the best time of his life—meant a lot to me."... Hoying went on to play seven years in the NFL with stints in Philadelphia and Oakland.

The Run-up

The "Domers" were coming to town, and that, alone, was enough motivation for quarterback Bob Hoying and his Ohio State teammates. Notre Dame—it's Golden Dome tradition.

Touchdown Jesus.

The luck of the Irish.

None of that seemed to matter.

"It was the most beautiful day you could imagine," Hoying remembers. "It was the perfect day for football. It felt like it was around 50 degrees, and it was sunny. There wasn't any wind—ideal from a quarterback's perspective."

Hoying said the crowd was instrumental in the Buckeyes' collective frame of mind. "During the bus ride from downtown Columbus to the stadium, we saw a huge traffic build-up. We hadn't played Notre Dame since the mid-1930s. It looked like there were 100,000 fans outside of the stadium. We were told after the game that thousands of fans who weren't able to make it into the stadium tailgated and partied outside."

With good reason—a victory against Notre Dame, anywhere and at any time, was worth its weight in, well … gold. This contest was a 45-26 shellacking of the Fighting Irish that seemed to be over before it began. OSU and Notre Dame don't play one another too often. When they do, the game's aura seems mightier than anything surrounding a game against Michigan.

Hoying said the hype for this game "… began the year before and carried through the summer. At some of the functions, when we were out and about around Columbus, people would talk about us playing Notre Dame in the fall. I think everyone got a sense it was just as big of a deal to our alumni … as it was to the players. We were all excited about the tradition of Notre Dame. It had been so long since we had played them that we knew this was going to be a special day. It was difficult during fall camp to keep our minds on our other games. Once we got to the week before the game, it was a relief to be able to concentrate on Notre Dame and give it our entire focus."

Ohio Stadium was jamming early, and he had a feeling it was going to be his day.

Bob Hoying made sure this game was "over" soon after it began.

"It was a perfect day to be a quarterback, no wind," Hoying recalled. "I remember in warmups looking forward to having a great day to play football in the stadium. We knew we were going to have the best opportunity to not only run the ball, but to throw the ball as well. They had a fairly hyped quarterback at the time, Ron Powlus, who [then-ESPN commentator] Beno Cook had predicted would win two Heisman trophies, when he was done at Notre Dame. [Luke] Fickell, [Mike] Vrable, [Matt] Finkes, and those guys were pretty much in his ear the entire game."

The Game

By Bob Hoying

Notre Dame at Ohio State—September 30, 1995

The outcome of a football game rarely is finalized until late in the contest, and even then it can be up for grabs. While I had other more personally rewarding games, if I had to relive a game it would be this one. I think it was late in the game, when victory was almost assured that we could appreciate what was happening.

We knew most of the fourth quarter that we were going to win that game. Being out on the field, being an Ohio kid, always wanting to play quarterback at Ohio State, and realizing you're about to beat Notre Dame in front of 100,000-plus at Ohio Stadium ... to have that all flash before your eyes [is what] sticks with me after all these years. This was also one of my better statistical games. I felt like I really contributed to that victory, like all of us out there on that field did. I think it was the fact that it was the perfect scenario for a perfect Saturday, against a formidable opponent that made this the game of my life.

The play that sticks out the most in my mind wasn't a special throw that I made, but it just a 12-yard end-around that Terry Glenn ran, and I threw it early in anticipation of him making the break. He caught it in full stride and outraced their defense for 80 yards for a touchdown. I remember sprinting as fast as I could to celebrate with him in the end zone. I was running down the field and watching him knowing that he was our fastest guy on the field and that no one was going to catch him. So I think about that play when I reflect on this.

I also think about the play with Eddie George outracing four or five defensive players. There's a photo of it that was replayed frequently when he won the Heisman. I think about those two plays more than any others.

I remember the first couple of series of the game. I was so anxious to play that I think I missed my first four or five throws. On a couple of occasions, I just overthrew it. I usually try to pride myself on being a poised and settled type of player, but it was such an electric day I remember being off the first two series. But then I settled down, and we won handily down the stretch.

I think the great thing about football is that you can be nervous, usually until you get hit the first time. Then the nervousness goes away, and you're just out there playing football like when you were in seventh or eighth grade, when you were just playing for fun. There can be a lot of hype before a game, but once you get your head knocked off the first time, it just brings you back down to earth, and you realize you're playing a football game, so you go about your business.

There was a big *Sports Illustrated* article on Ron Powlus before our game, and they had his girlfriend in there with pictures of them hanging out. And our defensive guys tried to get to him by talking trash. I won't repeat any of the particulars, but they tried to rattle him. At Ohio State, like at handful of schools, every game is important, but it was the fact that the alumni, everyone in town, and the players seemed to be waiting for this game. So it was great that everything went so well for me.

The Aftermath

The hype surrounding this game reminds Hoying of the hoopla in Ohio Stadium when Texas beat the Buckeyes 25-22 in 2005. He remembers the press' crush on this game. "Tons of media people were surrounding the field," he laughed. "I don't think they could have gotten another person in the stadium.

"If we weren't in the top five, it propelled us into the top five," Hoying said of the resounding victory. "We ended up being undefeated going into Michigan, and I think we were number two going into Michigan, so this kind of propelled us into the Big Ten season. We ended up pretty much winning handily through the Big Ten season until Michigan. It helped us to say we were one of the elite teams in the nation. It gave us a lot of confidence the rest of the year.

"It's a special experience after a game like that to share and unwind with your teammates and talk about what was going on. I do remember Coach [John] Cooper telling us that we would remember this game for the rest of our lives. He said something like, 'You're the first Ohio State team to beat Notre Dame.' I remember thinking that we did something pretty special."

It took some time for the initial luster to wear off, Hoying said. "For a couple of weeks, while you're walking across campus or are in the classroom, people that saw you congratulated you. We couldn't celebrate the victory too long because we had to move on to the next team."

Though this wasn't his greatest personal game or his greatest accomplishment, it was one of those "special games" that, as Cooper said, would never be forgotten. Therefore, it was the game of his life.

"The thing I most proud of was being voted captain my senior year," Hoying said. "That's very special to me, and I'm very proud of that. I'm also proud of winning the National Football Foundation's Vincent de Paul Draddy Award for the top scholar-athlete of all divisions of college football. I was shocked that I won it. It's not just football or academics, it takes into account all of your community work as well."

Hoying was preceded at Ohio State by another St. Henry alum, all-world tackle Jim Lachey. "I'm from the same high school as Jim, who was 10 years older than me, so when I was fourth, fifth, and sixth grade, I watched him play at Ohio State and then move on to the pros. My dream was to be a quarterback at Ohio State, I didn't even think of playing in the pros. I was looking at other schools only because Ohio State at the time was a run-saddled offense.

"I thought I was going to play basketball in college. I had some offers from Dayton, Bowling Green, Findlay, and places like that. I had a good year my junior year in high school with football and really started changing my mind as to what I wanted to do in college. I was Mr. Football in 1991, among other awards. It might have been the first time that someone from a small school won that award. I also played in the North-South All-Star Game. It was a big transition for me to go to a small rural school in western Ohio to 95,000 [fans] every Saturday. I always told people that Jim Lachey had done it before me, and Jim had been one of the best offensive linemen ever to play for Ohio State. I grew up with that and saw him live out his dream, I knew it was something that I could attain."

Today, Hoying is a principal in a partially eponymous firm.

"At Crawford Hoying Smith, we have a full-service real estate development and management company," he said. "We have fairly large multifamily developments and about 6,000 apartments that we own and manage. We also own condominiums. Additionally, we're a general contractor doing some of the bigger commercial projects in town. I feel very fortunate to be involved in something after football that makes me happy. I look forward to coming in every day and working hard and building something. I'm working with my dad and my brother, Tom, who played football with me at Ohio State. It's almost as fun as when I was playing football."

Hoying and his wife, Jill, have a son, Jacob, and a daughter, Ava. In his off-hours, he said he pursues golf and basketball, or stays busy "… just hanging out with the kids."

He wishes to be recalled as "… someone who poured out my heart and soul being the best teammate and quarterback I could. I was able to live out my dream. I was fortunate that I had great coaches and teammates. I'm disappointed that I played on very good teams, and it didn't work out that we beat Michigan during the two years we could have played for the national championship. We beat them my junior year, but we weren't in contention for the national championship that year. It wasn't for lack of effort on our part; it just didn't work out. I had a great opportunity to play with Eddie George, who won the Heisman that year—just a lot of great memories."

10

MIKE SENSIBAUGH

BIRTH DATE: January 3, 1949
HOMETOWN: Lockland, Ohio
RESIDENCE: Wildwood, Missouri
POSITION: Safety and punter
HEIGHT: 6 feet
WEIGHT: 187 pounds
YEARS: 1968 to 1970

Sensibaugh was All Southwest Ohio Player of the Year as a high school senior. ... His defensive backfield coach at OSU was Lou Holtz. ... He was an eighth-round draft pick in 1971 by the Kansas City Chiefs. ... Sensibaugh played freshman basketball at Ohio State. ... He holds the OSU career records for interceptions (22) and interception return yards (248).

The Run-up

Mike Sensibaugh was up against the mother lode of talent—on his own team.

"There were five defensive backs, including Jack Tatum," he said. "Our defensive backs coach, Lou Holtz, used us against each other. After our first game, he said he could not find me on film, so he benched me. The next game, [Mike] Polaski started as the free safety. In the Iowa and Michigan games, I wasn't used as a starter either. So going into the Rose Bowl, I wasn't sure if I would get to play that much. My dad was a minister, and his congregation raised enough money to send my whole family to watch me play in the Rose Bowl. I was nervous because I wasn't sure if I would get to play that much, and here I had my whole family watching.

"We weren't afraid of USC because we felt like we had taken care of the giants during our season—teams like Purdue [ranked No. 1 at the time] and Michigan. But, we knew we had to contain O.J. Simpson because we knew what kind of runner he was.

The Buckeyes, 10-0 and top-ranked going into the Rose Bowl, were unassuming and focused on Game Day.

"Prior to the game, we had special jerseys printed up so that they would show up nicely on television. However, because it was so hot, we decided to play in our junky old practice uniforms because the new ones were too warm. I remember the field was mostly dirt with hardly any grass."

The Game

By Mike Sensibaugh

No. 1 Ohio State vs. No. 2 Southern California
The Rose Bowl—January 1, 1969

Ted Provost got hurt in the first quarter, and I was sent in. O.J. had an 80-yard run, on which I was able to get a hand on him but couldn't stop him. However, we were able to stop O.J. at the goal line two times.

Mike Sensibaugh takes off on an interception return.

Prior to the game, we had scouted USC well. We noticed that O.J. had a tendency to run off-tackle and play the right side, which was my side. We had a pitch where all the linemen closed off the gaps. I scraped off-sides, so O.J. essentially ran right into my arms—twice. I guess they figured we wouldn't do it again.

We noticed in the USC-Notre Dame game that the Trojans liked to throw a deep pass. During one play, our rush was so good that the quarterback had a hard time getting off the pass. I intercepted the pass that was intended for Dickerson. I caught it on about the 20-yard line and ran it back about 50 yards—not because I was that fast, but because no one else was around.

We spotted them a 10-0 second-quarter lead before we were able to lock Simpson down for the rest of the game.

The Aftermath

Sensibaugh's best work in the Rose Bowl came on special teams, as he set school and Rose Bowl records by punting for 319 yards. Both records still stand. The Buckeyes' 27-16 victory ensured the team's place in history as the last Big Ten squad to win both the Associated Press and United Press International national championship rankings.

"It was pretty electrifying," said Sensibaugh. "In the locker room after the game, Holtz whistled to get our attention. O.J. walked in and said to us, 'You're the best.' I didn't find out until later that I set a Rose Bowl yardage record for punting. It was a great feeling, especially with my parents and four siblings being there. However, our coaches never let us really enjoy our victories. We always could have done something better. For example, while Holtz congratulated us on making the All-Bowl Team, he told us now we had to make the 'All-Ohio State' team."

There were many great days still ahead for Sensibaugh. He was part of another national championship team in 1970, after the Buckeyes, again, won the Big Ten. After being named first-team All-America, he was drafted in 1971 by the Kansas City Chiefs. He went on to pick off 27 passes in eight years as a safety with the Chiefs and St. Louis Cardinals.

Sensibaugh stayed in Missouri after his playing days were complete. While he's owned and operated a swimming-pool business since the late 1970s, he said that's not his true vocation.

"While I was playing football, I couldn't indulge my bird-hunting hobby because they both took place during the same season," he said. "But, being in the pool business, the seasons are opposite, so now I get to hunt as much as I want. In fact, you could say I'm in the 'bird-hunting business,' with a pool hobby on the side."

Sensibaugh's fondest football memories come from that 1968 team.

"I was recruited as a quarterback, but like a lot of the guys who made up the 'Super Sophomores' group, I knew there would be a lot of rearranging. Bruce Jankowski was the leading running back in New Jersey. When he came to Ohio State, he became a wide receiver. Everyone took what was on the table—no pouting. As a freshman, I played only two games. We spent the rest of the season practicing with the varsity. If we thought we were something coming in, that notion quickly changed. We had a lot of great athletes able to change positions and make things work. In addition to the sophomores not playing the positions that we thought we were, the seniors also were put in different positions. They showed real leadership and stepped up like everyone else.

"Our 1968 team was special," Sensibaugh added warmly. "So I'd like to be remembered as one of the guys on that squad who was able to adapt to the needs of the team."

11

PANDEL SAVIC

BIRTH DATE: July 15, 1925
HOMETOWN: Gerard, Ohio
RESIDENCE: Dublin, Ohio
POSITION: Quarterback/Linebacker
HEIGHT: 6-foot-1
WEIGHT: 196 pounds
YEARS: 1947 to 1949

Savic joined the U.S. Marine Corps in 1943 despite having already landed a scholarship to Ohio State. ... He is a veteran of the battles for Pela Lu and Okinawa. ... After World War II, he chose Ohio State over Platoon Commander School. ... Savic led the team to the 1950 Rose Bowl, where Ohio State beat California 17-14. ... He later helped start the Muirfield Village Golf Club and Muirfield Tournament with his good friend, Jack Nicklaus.

Pandel Savic also guided Ohio State to a Rose Bowl victory against the University of California-Berkeley.

The Run-up

By the time that the Rose Bowl became the game for the winners of the Big Ten and the Pac-8, Michigan had become a conference powerhouse. Ohio State had gotten close to Pasadena a few times before, but never quite there. For Buckeye quarterback Pandel Savic, his last game against Michigan was his last chance to make that trip.

"We had to tie or win to go to the Rose Bowl. Michigan had gone to the Rose Bowl the previous year and could not go again," he said. "We prepared for Michigan like we always prepared. They were the top contender."

Savic was determined to have the Buckeyes' single-wing offense ready for the Wolverines. "The coaches could not send in plays from the bench. I had to study my opponents, their strengths and their weaknesses, the field conditions, the wind. My teammates always told me what they wanted to do, what plays they wanted to run. I was good at listening to them."

The Game
By Pandel Savic

Ohio State at Michigan—November 19, 1949

Michigan had a hard-charging tackle, Al Wistert, who was ... formidable. ... Our team started double-teaming, hitting him hard. We wanted to knock him out of the game, and we did. They were ahead 7-0.

Trailing by a touchdown, we had to capitalize on Wistert's absence, so I went to the air.

I faked to our fullback, spun around, and faked to our halfback. Our opponents thought I was going to run at this point—especially since we had been running most of the game. The linebackers were frozen. So, I threw the ball for about 45 yards to our wing-back, Ray

Hamilton. He was around the 5-yard line. On the next play, we pushed across the goal line.

The score was now 7-6, Michigan. We kicked the extra point, but it was blocked. I looked up, and they were calling Michigan for offsides, so we got a second chance—and we tied up the ball game.

It was Hell for the last two to three minutes of the game, but we preserved the tie, which earned us the Rose Bowl bid.

The Aftermath

"Obviously we were very happy," Savic said. "They brought us roses into the training room for us to hold and kiss. We knew we were going to the Rose Bowl, and that this was a first for Ohio State."

The atmosphere was one of mutual appreciation—for one another and for what had been accomplished coming out of a period in our nation's history that was, as times, as nail-biting as this game was.

"A lot of us had gone off to war before coming to Ohio State, so this was a nice outcome," he added. "For a lot of us, it was just great to make the football team, see pretty girls, and concentrate on making good grades. We really wanted to further ourselves. I think perhaps it meant more to us."

Savic went into the industrial safety business with 1948 OSU football captain David Templeton. He took it over in 1984, and, in 1999, he sold the company. He married and had two daughters along the way.

The octogenarian can still shoot his age on the golf course and helps to organize Jack Nicklaus' golf tournament, The Memorial, as chairman emeritus of the board. He also enjoys classical music and painting, often at his winter home in Florida.

The victory against Michigan was the high point of his OSU career, he said, but he wants to be remembered for other things.

"The man I've become from my early years, my personal traits that I hold dearly come from serving in the United States Marine Corps and playing OSU football," Savic explained. "I gained my discipline, my strengths from these [experiences]. I'd like to be remembered as a kind man who always brought up a question and solved some problems. While I wasn't the most adept at throwing, it didn't matter as much because we weren't a passing team. However, I'd like to be remembered for listening to the other players and leading them as best I could."

12

RICK MIDDLETON

BIRTH DATE: November 28, 1951
HOMETOWN: Delaware, Ohio
RESIDENCE: Columbus, Ohio
POSITION: Linebacker
HEIGHT: 6-foot-3
WEIGHT: 222 pounds
YEARS: 1971 to 1973

A first-round draft pick of the New Orleans Saints in 1974 (one pick before teammate Randy Gradishar was taken by the Denver Broncos), Middleton also played for the San Diego Chargers.

The Run-up

Rick Middleton said it was an "electric" setting, "… as it always was in Ohio Stadium against Michigan." This one was for the Big Ten Conference championship and trip to the Rose Bowl. Michigan was ranked No. 1 in the nation at the time, too—another Michigan game, another season-ending showdown.

The Buckeyes, mirroring Coach Woody Hayes' demeanor, were steeled, ready for the challenge.

"All during the week, Woody brought in players who were hurt and could not play," Middleton recalled. "They all said the same thing: how much they wanted to play, what a great honor it was to be able to play in the Michigan game, how lucky we were. Several were crying or on the verge of crying. We did the same thing that we usually did pregame. The night before we had dinner at the [Ohio State] golf course, followed by a movie. It was probably *Billy Jack*, because we saw that at least 20 times. The story was that at one time, Woody had shown a movie that wasn't action-packed, and the team lost. So, we got to watch *Billy Jack* all the time."

Middleton said at the pregame breakfast the next day, the feeling that this was *the* game began to spread throughout the dining room. It just escalated.

"While we were getting ready in the locker room, some crazy, drugged-out guy flew through it," Middleton said. "The cops came running through trying to catch him. They had a hard time getting control of him. It pretty much reflected our mood and set the mood for the game—crazy, violent, and wild."

The Game
By Rick Middleton

Michigan at Ohio State—November 24, 1972

Any time you play a Michigan game it was different from all the other games you would be in during your playing years. During the

1972 game, our two teams were fighting it out for the Big Ten Championship once again. It was the fifth meeting between Bo and Woody, and we were still angry about the loss the year before. The 1971 game was a classic as our undermanned Buckeye team played Michigan toe to toe and nearly won. Woody had a temper tantrum on the sideline because of a disputed call, and everyone was looking forward to the rematch. It was on national television, a game of national prominence. The intensity level for the game was as high as it could possibly be.

Our defensive coordinator, George Hill, had us practicing goal-line defenses throughout the year, and we were very proud of that defense. You hope to be able to stop a team and force them to punt each time, but invariably, you will have to use it during some games. We had three great goal-line stands during that 1972 game and held them on four downs several other times during the game. That, along with other factors, helped our three linebackers become the ABC Defensive Players of the Game. It was a shining moment for the defense as a whole and for me, personally.

During the first stand, Michigan was on the two-yard line, on either second or third down. We had Michigan well scouted, and our defensive scheme was to angle and have the linebackers shoot the gaps. Their quarterback dropped the ball and quickly recovered it, but it wouldn't have mattered as I had already crashed in and tackled Chuck Heater, their tailback. On the next play, Pete Cusick slammed into their fullback, and I helped bring him down for no gain. After another play for no gain, we took over on our 1-yard line without giving up a point.

During our second goal-line stand, the Michigan fullback, Ed Shuttlesworth, who was from Ohio, tried to run, but I was able to hit him head on and stop that run. (Linebacker) Arnie Jones was all over the field throughout the game and had some great tackles as well. In fact, Arnie was credited with about 20 tackles for the game, while I was given around 18, and Randy Gradishar had about 15.

During the fourth quarter, Michigan was at midfield and running out of time and downs. We called a blitz, which was very rare for us. I went through the guard-tackle gap and dropped the fullback for a

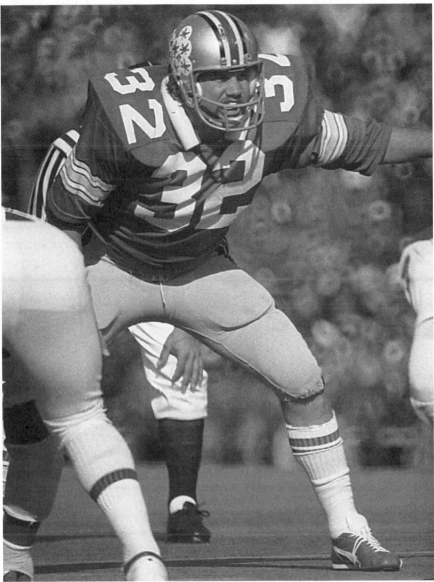

A "coach" on the field, Rick Middleton barks orders for the defense.

three-yard loss. In one of Woody's books, I am proud to say that he mentioned that play in his description of situations where someone rose to the occasion to make the great play at a desperate time. I am extremely proud that Coach Hayes thought so highly of my effort. During the last tackle of the game (defensive tackle) George Hasenohrl sacked (Michigan quarterback) Dennis Franklin for a loss to end their drive. After he nailed him, he patted him on the head, and the stadium went crazy.

Our offense did a great job as well. Quarterback Greg Hare, a very underrated player, had a 20- to 30-yard run, which was beautiful to watch. Woody would later use that run to show what he meant when he described a runner leaving the defenders on the ground like a string of pearls. Greg left about seven or eight Michigan defenders behind him as he made them miss tackle after tackle on that run. His run opened the defense up a bit, which led to (tailback) Archie Griffin's long run for a touchdown that put us ahead for good.

The Aftermath

The 14-12 victory over the previously ranked No. 1 Wolverines earned the Buckeyes exactly what they wanted—a trip to Pasadena.

"After the game I was literally physically and emotionally exhausted, and for the second time that year I had to be assisted to the training room after the game," Middleton said. "A bit later, Woody came in and congratulated me for my efforts and gave me the game ball. I still have that game ball, and I am very proud of the picture of me holding that ball while sitting on the training room table that appeared in *The Columbus Dispatch* the next day. I believe that Woody gave me the ball for several reasons. I did play well that day, but so did others.

"The thing that I really prided myself in was never quitting, and never allowing anyone else on my team to quit either. A lot of the good things that I did as a player occurred in our huddle, or on the sideline when I was talking to my teammates. Being a good player is one thing, but helping to make others to be good players is something that I prided myself in doing. I think that something my dad once told me helped me to be the player that I was. He told me after a game in high school that he really didn't care about the outcome of the game. He just wanted me to '… play as hard as you can, and as well as you can, for as long as you can.' I strove to make my dad proud every time that I was on the field. In this game, I came as close to doing that as I possibly could."

The victory brought on a feeling of euphoria, Middleton said, and the reality of what he had accomplished brought more than a game ball.

"In previous games, ABC had given one scholarship to a school in the name of two or three players when they were picked as the player of the game," he said. "When this game was over, ABC, for the first time, gave out a scholarship in each of our names for our work on the defensive side of the ball. We were also named the UPI Players of the Week the following week. A number of my friends called to congratulate me, but there really wasn't any celebration. We just went back to practice because we had the Rose Bowl coming up."

Middleton said his on-field exploits were known, and he's proud of them, but fond memories are of out-of-action contributions to the whole notion of "team," too.

"Mostly, I remember the things I did on the sidelines, during the huddle, in the locker room. For example, in my junior year, we had a sit-down strike. One of the players had missed some meetings, and Woody was very angry. He said he was throwing him off the team. Several of us thought that this was too harsh and decided to 'strike.' Instead of going out to practice, we stayed in the locker room. Woody came in. He could hypnotize you and make you think whatever he wanted you to think. I spoke up to Woody and said what he was doing was wrong. He had guys who were scared to death that they might make a mistake and that he would go ballistic—especially on offense. He was much more civilized to the guys on defense. Woody said, 'Okay, you've given me a lot to think about,' and walked out. The [player] didn't get kicked off. [Linebacker] Vic Koegel came up to me afterwards and said he would vote for me for captain."

Middleton's journey to OSU was something of destiny.

"My mom and dad both went to Ohio State," he explained. "My grandmother lived north of campus, and when we visited, my parents would sell parking spaces during the games, and my brother and I would sell buckeyes—for a quarter, I think. I didn't really think about going anywhere other than OSU. I went on a visit to Michigan in 1979, because OSU was playing them up there that year. When OSU lost, I was furious because I was already identifying myself as part of that team. I never really thought about playing professional football even though I was a Browns fan. I always thought about playing college football, especially for Ohio State, even though in those days they hardly televised any college football games. We were lucky if we could get a rebroadcast on WOSU-TV of the previous day's Buckeye game."

At Delaware Hayes High School, where Middleton followed in his brother's steps, he was a three-year letterman in football, basketball, and baseball.

"My sophomore year I was a defensive back," he said. "My junior year I switched to tight end and linebacker. My senior year I was All-State. I was chosen by the Columbus Touchdown Club as the Governor Rhodes Player of the Year."

Middleton just completed his 25th year as a government teacher at Olentangy High School in suburban Columbus, and he also has become a psychology teacher. He recently gave up coaching.

He and his wife, Debbie, are approaching their 25th wedding anniversary. They have two children. "My wife and I love to travel with the kids all over the country. We drove out to Yellowstone Park one year. I've also enjoyed coaching my kids' teams."

His OSU football legacy?

"I would like to be remembered for what I did for the team, not only on the field, but on the sidelines, always congratulating the offense when they came off the field, cheerleading the players on the field, and mediating when necessary," Middleton said. "I'd like to be remembered as the guy who made the team better."

13

TIM ANDERSON

BIRTH DATE: November 22, 1980
HOMETOWN: Clyde, Ohio
RESIDENCE: Buffalo, New York
POSITION: Defensive tackle
HEIGHT: 6-foot-4
WEIGHT: 289 pounds
YEARS: 2000 to 2003

He was high school Lineman of the Year for Northwestern Ohio his junior and senior years. ... He was twice a state wrestling champion. ... "It was a tough decision on whether to play football or wrestle," he said. "Several Division I schools recruited me to do one or the other. I had to pick the sport with the most promising future. With football I knew my career didn't have to end after college; with wrestling, the only post-college opportunity was the Olympics." ... Anderson is entering his third season with the Buffalo Bills of the NFL.

Despite clearly being held by a Miami lineman, Tim Anderson nearly gets Ken Dorsey for a sack in the Fiesta Bowl.

The Run-Up

The 2003 Fiesta Bowl was the national championship game. Miami, the defending champion and owner of a 34-game winning streak, was an 11½ point favorite over the Buckeyes, according to the national media—or at least that's how Tim Anderson thought the media was playing it.

"Sportswriters and commentators predicted the game would be over by halftime. There was an ESPN correspondent who said we'd lose by 40 points; however, those of us on the team and the coaching staff knew we could beat them," Anderson proclaimed. "Our victory was that much sweeter because of all of those saying we couldn't do it. Plus, the game was on the national stage."

The pregame routine was pretty much the same as the previous 13 games, but this wasn't just any game.

"The media were everywhere," he said. "Everyone wanted to interview us. We noticed former Buckeyes who were now playing in the NFL, as well as non-Buckeye NFL players such as Warren Sapp. It was pretty cool to see them walking around the field. I remember sitting in the locker room for at least a half an hour waiting for the game to start. Some of us even took off our shoulder pads because we were getting too hot. By the time we finally got out on the field, it seemed like we had to warm up again after sitting and waiting for so long. Our muscles had started to tighten up."

The Game

By Tim Anderson

Ohio State vs. Miami (Florida)
The Fiesta Bowl—January 3, 2003

I heard the trash talk personally from Miami's center, Brett Romberg. He had a reputation as a crazy guy. I had heard he had sunbathed on their field in his jock strap—and nothing but his jock strap. He had been making comments about me all week, saying that he was going to be pinching my butt. His strategy was to try to frustrate us mentally, so he could beat us physically. I had to restrain myself and not return his comments, which was hard. I knew I had to let my performance speak for itself.

We played really well and led most of the game. We had a sack on the first play. After that sack, Miami's offensive line just sort of looked at each other. It was almost as if we had taken them by surprise. They seemed to be thinking that our guys actually might be good. After that play, they were shooting from the hip. I was able to get a couple of nice shots on Miami's quarterback Ken Dorsey and did get several sacks.

The rest of the game was a blur—a wonderful 31-24 winning national championship blur. With a game like that, it's hard to remember all the personal plays, although there is a tendency to remember the ones in which I felt like I could have done better. For example, I remember when I was in pursuit of Willis McGahee, and he ducked. I couldn't stop, so I went flying over him. Although I wasn't able to stop him, I slowed him down enough for my teammates to get him. It was like that throughout the whole game—everyone stepped up to the plate. McGahee is now one of my teammates with the Bills, and I try not to let him forget about the game.

The Aftermath

Anderson said it's "surreal" to think about being on the winning side of one of the greatest games in college football history. "It's hard to put into words. It was one of the best feelings I've ever had. The locker room was crazy. We couldn't stop smiling. I celebrated with my teammates, friends, and family. Immediately after the game, I had an interview with Dom Tiberi from Channel 10 in Columbus. He asked me about the comments Romberg had been making all week about pinching my butt. I responded that I didn't think he had time because I was too busy whupping his ass."

Only one thing could possibly match that big win.

"I'd have to say that getting my degree was on par with winning the National Championship," Anderson beamed. "When I was growing up in a small town, I wasn't expecting to go to college. Getting my degree was also my parents' biggest goal for me. So as amazing as that game was, getting my degree was equally important."

In Anderson's spare time, he enjoys golfing, hunting, fishing, watching NASCAR, and spending time with his bull mastiff.

Anderson is unsure of his imprint on Ohio State football.

"I don't know if I'll always be remembered as an OSU football great. I hope that the group of guys that I played with, the coaches, and the real fans who knew me believed that I was tough, hardworking, and disciplined. I hope that Coach [Jim] Heacock, my positions coach, saw me as an overachiever, not an underachiever. I hope that I'm remembered for doing the right things: always striving to improve my performance, putting the team first, and being a good leader. I hope that I never caused anyone problems, or that anyone held a negative opinion of me."

14

DICK MACK

BIRTH DATE: December 21, 1953
HOMETOWN: Bucyrus, Ohio
RESIDENCE: Avon Lake, Ohio
POSITION: Offensive guard
HEIGHT: 5-foot-11
WEIGHT: 217 pounds
YEARS: 1972 to 1974

Mack served as a graduate assistant for Woody Hayes. ... He grew up a Michigan fan, but didn't receive a scholarship offer because he was considered too small to play offensive line in the Big Ten Conference.

The Run-up

The Buckeyes had waited all year for a Rose Bowl rematch against USC, after getting hammered 42-17 in the 1973 game against the Trojans. Accentuating the hard feelings was a late-season tie with Michigan, which almost cost OSU's 10-0-1 squad a return visit to Pasadena.

"After our tie with Michigan, we had lost our motivation," he said. "We didn't know, at first, if we would be going to the Rose Bowl. We had played there the previous year and lost badly. We could return this year because this was the first year the no-repeat rule was no longer in effect. The Big Ten athletic directors voted the Sunday after the Michigan game as to who would go to Pasadena."

The thirst for revenge was so strong that Woody Hayes was forced to change his game plan.

"We were all anticipating a chance to redeem ourselves," Mack claimed. "Redemption and retribution would be our theme, given our performance the previous year. During our practices leading up to the game, the coaching staff rebelled and forced Woody to work on our passing game. In practice, we would work on throwing the ball, but still only passed the ball a half dozen times. We knew we could win if Woody let us pass more. But we also knew it would be a dogfight. We had our normal warmup procedures; but, because it was pregame, we notched our hitting up a bit."

The Game

By Dick Mack

Ohio State vs. USC
The Rose Bowl—January 1, 1974

The emphasis on the passing game paid off as everyone, except Hayes, predicted.

Dick Mack is off and running in pass-protection mode.

We started out trying to throw the ball, and we completed seven-of-nine passes, which was enough to open up Southern Cal's defense because they couldn't put 11 men on the line of scrimmage.

It was a tight contest and was close at halftime. Our hitting was tremendous, though, and we felt like we were going to win.

I made the play of my life right before halftime. We were on the goal line, and John Hicks, an emotional man, was our right tackle. He was second in the Heisman vote that year. On the other side, playing for USC was Gary Jeter, a Cleveland native who lived across the street from Hicks. Across from me was Richard Wood, who we called "Batman." He was a three-time All-America linebacker and very fast.

On our next play, Hicks buried Jeter into the ground, and I buried Wood on the goal line in what became the best block of my life. We had carved an opening for our fullback, Pete Johnson, who waltzed across the goal line to score.

We owned the second half. Archie Griffin broke half a dozen tackles on one play. We really overpowered them and had the feeling of having them on the run. When we went over to the bench, we didn't have to worry about one missed block—we were able to relax and watch the game. The momentum really changed early in the third quarter, and we started to exert our will. We ran away with the game.

It was particularly gratifying for me because my brother had played for Michigan in the mid-'60s. He used to rub it in to me that he had been on a winning team, and now I was able to give it back to him. I had been fortunate to watch him win the Rose Bowl in person, and because he was playing for the Rams in 1974, he and the rest of my family were able to watch me play in Pasadena.

The Aftermath

The Buckeyes celebrated their win the way college guys generally do.

"I remember lots of partying," he said. "We had been staying at the Huntington Hotel in Pasadena, which was well beyond its youthful years. It wasn't conducive to 20-year-olds, so we went to parties in Pasadena. As a 19-year-old kid, I was on top of the world. We felt vindicated. We hadn't been successful in the Rose Bowl for a while, but had been 10-0-1 that year. We were hopeful to be national champions, but ended up second in the country behind Notre Dame. I was thrilled with everyone's performance during the game."

However, for Mack, that game was a small part of his Ohio State legacy.

"I guess being able to earn two degrees while playing football, being part of the greatest athletic program, and being around Coach Hayes were my greatest accomplishments."

Mack moved on to the business world after football.

"I've been in the trust business for 25 years," he said. "I'm a senior fiduciary officer for National City Bank, and I'm using my law degree to manage litigation.

"I was widowed and a single dad for six years. I married my son's preschool teacher. I now have four children. My oldest is 25, and I have a 16-year-old, a 12-year-old, and a nine-year-old."

15

GREG FREY

BIRTH DATE: January 29, 1968
HOMETOWN: Cincinnati, Ohio
RESIDENCE: Columbus, Ohio
POSITION: Quarterback
HEIGHT: 6-foot-2
WEIGHT: 195 pounds
YEARS: 1986 to 1991

Greg was featured as a Sports Illustrated *"Face in the Crowd" as a senior at St. Xavier High School in Cincinnati after throwing for 486 yards against the vaunted Cincinnati Moeller team. ... Grew up a Notre Dame fan. ... Played on Big Ten championship teams in football (1986) and baseball (1991), earning six varsity letters in the process—four in football, two in baseball. ... Columbus Touchdown Club Scholar Athlete of the Year 1990 ... was only QB in Ohio State history to throw for 2,000 yards in three consecutive seasons. ... The Detroit Tigers drafted him in 1991. ... He played with the Ohio Glory in the World Football League and the Cleveland Thunderbolts in the Arena Football League.*

The Run-up

The Hubert H. Humphrey Metrodome wasn't at capacity, but it had the capacity to be loud. It was a typical road game, with a nice mix of home fans and, as always, the boisterous, noisy Buckeye faithful who made the trip.

"Our routine was pretty much the same before all of our games. I don't remember much, but I do remember that I felt great during the warmup. I felt like I was in a rhythm. However, the feelings I had before warmup weren't always indicative of how the game would go. Sometimes warmups felt perfect, yet the game would go horribly wrong, and sometimes the opposite would happen as well."

The Game

By Greg Frey

Ohio State at Minnesota—October 28, 1989

Minnesota jumped out to a 31-0 lead before the first half was over. In the first half, 99 percent of everything went Minnesota's way, and everything we did went wrong. We had six turnovers that day, five in the first half. Our offense, our defense, and our special teams all performed poorly in that first half. Minnesota scored almost immediately off of one of our turnovers. They followed that with a field goal and scored a touchdown after that.

It was 17-0 before we got the ball into scoring position. On a third-and-goal at the Golden Gophers' 8-yard line, offensive coordinator Jim Colletto called a toss-sweep to set up a chip-shot field goal attempt. I went into the huddle believing we should be thinking a touchdown, but he was thinking field goal. He wanted to get something on the board. I wanted something bigger.

Once we broke the huddle and got to the line of scrimmage, Jeff Graham was one-on-one on the right side, which was his green light to check to a fade route. I decided to change the play and go for the

Greg Frey engineered one of the most amazing comebacks in OSU history.

TD. However, I needed 10 guys to hear the change, and given the crowd noise, only nine did. The crowd was loud, and Jeff Davidson, who somehow played the entire game with a separated shoulder, thought we were going with the toss-sweep and pulled to the right side like he was supposed to do on a sweep.

I took the snap and went to throw the ball to Graham, when the free safety swept through untouched and obliterated me as I was setting my feet to throw to Jeff. One of their guys, Shawn Lumpkin, I think, intercepted the ball for a 92-yard touchdown.

So then it was 24-0, not 17-3 or 17-7, and I was lying on the ground. My head was dinged, and I was feeling pretty woozy. Plus, I had to walk to the sidelines to get chewed out by my coach. My head hurt, my feelings were hurt, and there was dissension on the field because Davidson did not hear me. It was one of those "When it rains, it pours" moments.

We got the ball back with three minutes left in the first half. We went three-and-out on our drive, which gave Minnesota another turn. On our punt, they wound up with 12 guys on the field. We ended up with a first-down gift, courtesy of Minnesota.

We got the ball back and were able to make it inside the five. Carlos Snow ran over a Minnesota linebacker and made it into the end zone on fourth down. We went for two, and I hit Jeff Graham for the two extra points, to get the score to 31-8 at halftime.

(Ohio State managed three two-point conversions in the game.)

It was an amazing turnaround for us mentally. In the locker room, I told my teammates that we could beat Minnesota. I reminded them that we weren't playing Michigan—that it was just Minnesota. I also reminded them that we were capable of doing to Minnesota what they had just done to us. We were organized, positive, and controlled.

We opened the second half with a 96-yard drive that resulted in a field goal. The drive chewed up a lot of time, but it was important to us because we put some more points on the board. The third quarter moved kind of slowly. I think it ended 31-18, but our momentum had shifted as we began accumulating points.

With just five minutes left in the fourth quarter, they were still very much in control with a 37-27 lead. Our last two drives were critical. After a touchdown pass to Jim Palmer was called back, I hit Graham with a perfect strike to set up fourth-and-goal at the 1-yard line. I then ran an option keeper into the end zone to cut the lead to 37-34.

We got the ball back with like two minutes left in the game. Colletto was expecting Minnesota to use a two-deep, man-under coverage. ... We had to go 80 yards and, sure enough, they did what we expected. I hit Carlos Snow, who was wide open, for 20 or 25 yards. He went out of bounds to stop the clock. On the second play, Minnesota stayed in their man-under two-deep. ... I stayed in the pocket and was able to get a pass off to Brian Stablein for about an 18-yard gain.

Two plays later, I committed the mortal sin of taking a sack. We lost 13 yards, and the clock kept ticking. It was a killer mistake, and we were in a state of chaos, which is typical of a two-minute drill.

On the next play, I scrambled to my left and hit Jim Palmer. He made the catch at about 10 yards and broke a couple of tackles to take the ball deep in Minnesota territory for a 34-yard gain. He made what was probably his biggest play of his life at a time when his team desperately needed a big play.

On our last play, we had two receivers split right, with Graham on the inside. Bobby Olive ran a five-yard hitch, and Graham ran a post corner. Minnesota lined up with man-to-man coverage. I was supposed to fake to our running back, but I was so confident that Jeff would be open that I just took my drop and lofted the ball toward the corner of the end zone. Jeff made an amazing move, and the free safety had no chance.

The irony was, it was the easiest throw of the game, but it was for the winning touchdown. I took my helmet off and threw my hands in the air, which was out of character for me.

The Aftermath

The extra point made the score 41-37, with less than a minute left, capping off an amazing 41-6 comeback.

"That was the game of my life for a variety of reasons, but mostly because it became a defining moment in my life," Frey recalled. "The game was littered with life lessons on how to handle adversity. I was blessed to be able to relate it to my life; although the adversity we face in football pales in comparison to the adversity we face in life. It was a reminder that—no matter how bad things get, that with guts, composure, and faith—you can always turn things around.

"It's difficult to describe the feeling, but it was a mixture of relief and celebration. What was nice about winning on the road is that you get to share it first with just your teammates. That night we arrived back in Columbus and went out on campus to celebrate. Everyone we met congratulated us and said they were in shock that we actually pulled it off. I still meet people who come up to me and tell me where they were that day. I never get tired of hearing those stories."

Frey is a now a commercial realtor in Columbus for Crawford Hoying Smith, but he remains close to the gridiron. He is offensive coordinator for Bexley High School and does the Columbus Destroyers' games for Fox Sports Ohio, as well as some high school games. He also turns up on the radio covering Buckeye football. He spends his spare time golfing, skiing, or playing with his two golden retrievers.

Frey said that day in Minnesota is his legacy.

"I would like to be remembered as a quarterback who produced some great moments for the Ohio State fans all over the world, and as a guy who never quit despite the score or the odds. Most people remember me for the Minnesota game, and I feel very lucky to have been a part of that Buckeye team on that day."

16

JAN WHITE

BIRTH DATE: October 6, 1948
HOMETOWN: Harrisburg, Pennsylvania
RESIDENCE: Clayton, Ohio
POSITION: Tight end
HEIGHT: 6-foot-2
WEIGHT: 212 pounds
YEARS: 1968 to 1970

White was drafted by the Buffalo Bills of the NFL, the 30th selection overall in 1971. ... White played in the NFL for two years. ... Originally invited to play in the former College All-Star game, which pitted college standouts against the defending Super Bowl champions, White opted out after his agent advised against it. ... During his three-year Ohio State career, White had 61 receptions for 762 yards; for perspective, in today's climate that is an average season for a wide receiver.

Jan White, who says he initially didn't want to play tight end, ultimately became an All-American at that position.

The Run-up

Ladies and gentlemen, say hello to the eventual All-America tight end who didn't want to be one—but hold that thought.

Jan White remembers the possibility of a letdown in this game. After all, Ohio State, which entered the season ranked No. 11 by the wire service polls, the week before had knocked off—make that spanked—then-No. 1-rated Purdue in Ohio Stadium. The *Sports Illustrated* cover headline, "Bye, Bye No. 1" spoke volumes. White was one among the vaunted "Super Sophs"—perhaps the best recruiting class of all time at Ohio State, and certainly one of the best ever assembled nationally.

"They were calling us the Baby Bucks, but at that point, we weren't freshmen anymore," White said. "We had between 11 and 13 sophomores starting."

About that letdown—the Buckeyes certainly were ripe for it. Coming off the most stunning upset to that point in school football history, Ohio State was elevated to No. 2 in the nation. Fat heads? It clearly was a possibility.

"There was concern in the locker room," White recalls, "not from the coaches, necessarily, but from the players. We really were concerned about a letdown. We had the abilities on this team to beat the No. 1 team in the nation. Even I was questioning us: 'Just how good are we?'"

At this point in his young career, it is important to note, White was converted to tight end from wide receiver. "There was an injury, and they decided to move me inside. I kept thinking, 'I don't want to be [a tight end], are you kidding me? Isn't there someone else better?'

"All of a sudden, I'm part of Woody Hayes' running game," he said. "Mind you, all I did in high school was play wide receiver. I was a speed guy. So now I'm in the running game next to [Rufus] Mayes and [Dave] Foley, two great tackles at the top of their game then, although by today's standards they couldn't compare. We called them the 'Twin Towers,' and I was always afraid they were going to step on me. I was not big at all. What I was, though, was really fortunate. I learned quickly what I needed to do and I learned it well. They're bigger [the defensive linemen] and they hit harder, so you have to hit them first. They didn't know our cadence or when the ball would be snapped. I became mentally prepared. Woody used to say, 'If you're going to fight in the North Atlantic, then you should train in the North Atlantic.' I guess my training at tight end was my North Atlantic."

There was a ton of excitement in Ohio Stadium on game day. "They were all wondering, too, 'How good are these guys?' Did we sneak up on Purdue? I don't think so. I can tell you this about the Purdue game: Purdue didn't want to come out after halftime. We had lost big to them the year before. We were all freshmen then, just standing around watching. I think in '68, they didn't take us all that seriously—until they saw what we were made of."

The night before the game, the Buckeyes were cloistered in a Columbus hotel. "We always stayed at the same hotel, and we always ate at the Jai Lai [the former Columbus restaurant, Hayes' favorite, on whose site now sits the Buckeye Hall of Fame Café]," White explained. "I remember the locker room that day. There were certain guys who were always quiet, going over their assignments for the game and conserving their energy. Some were wild-eyed; you could sense the testosterone aura, and they were ready to break a locker over their heads. They were champing at the bit. Others were more intellectual about it; they wanted to review the plays, study the audibles, and remember the audible calls. Others listened to music. We were different individuals, but we were a team. I remember when the trainer was taping me for the game, I told him, 'Put a touchdown into that for me.'"

Again, White said the Buckeyes weren't overconfident. "We did not know then what we were made of, and we had no clue whatsoever how good we were. Even if we did, Woody wouldn't have allowed it. If he sensed it, we would have been in deep doo-doo. He would have worked us to the bone! I was so happy to be there—in the Big Ten with a chance to go to the Rose Bowl."

Little did he and his teammates know.

The Game

By Jan White

Northwestern at Ohio State—October 19, 1968

We got off to a really good lead. I scored my very first touchdown, and I went 72 yards. My knees were shaking. What did I know about playing tight end? But the play was called from the huddle. I thought, "Oh, my gosh; it's coming to me."

I was reading the defense coming up to the line, knowing I was going to get a shove or a bump from the linebacker. There was a lot running through my mind, but I wanted the ball. Rex Kern threw me a 12- to 14-yard pass, and I had run a good post pattern. I'm thinking to myself, I have to go get this thing, because Woody always said that when you pass the ball, three things can happen and two of them are bad. That much was ingrained. Nobody sensed the fear in my eyes!

I thought I would just throw a couple blocks, roll around and get dirty, but then there was the ball, heading towards me. I thought, "I'd better not get caught."

I beat coverage, which was a zone. I went underneath the safety. When I had come off the line, Northwestern's linebacker on that side pushed me. Then I noticed the safety move into zone (coverage), so I made my post move, and it was a routine pass. Once I caught it, I could see where the cornerback was, and he was watching (flanker) Bruce Jankowski. It became a footrace that I was determined to win. It was incredible. The only chance there was of me not scoring on that play was if I had fallen down. I had enough confidence in my speed—I was a state record-holder in track in high school—but you just never know.

Once I was into the end zone, I don't remember everything that happened, but I do remember that the crowd was just ecstatic. Remember, we didn't throw the ball that much.

Playing tight end became a matter of survival in the beginning. Former athletic director Hugh Hindman was my position coach. He had the ends and tackles. He said he had a lot of confidence in me. I remember thinking, "Are you kidding me?" I was not adept. I told him, "Maybe you should think about somebody else." I wasn't interested in blocking!

I figured I would just stay out there and stay out of the way. But he said to me, "My philosophy is you're an athlete. Would I ask you to do this if we didn't feel you could do it?" Patience; that's what he taught me.

I was an All-American as a senior, so I guess it worked out.

The Aftermath

White experienced a euphoric feeling at the final gun. Not only had his team won another game—one many thought would be played in letdown mode coming off the upset of Purdue—but he also had his first touchdown in his hip pocket.

"I remember I was on Cloud Nine," he said. "It was not just my first touchdown, but a 72-yard touchdown—and I didn't get caught! Oh, boy … it was just an awesome feeling. I was trying not to be too cocky, because I knew with our offense I might never see the ball again. Humility is part of who I am. Being humble is a good quality. My parents [Lewis and Rachel] taught me that, and they taught me well. When you're unsure of yourself, and you have four weeks to learn a new position, something like this game can be a great confidence booster. I savored the moment—for the moment. The following Monday, I moved on."

Truth be told, had Jan White followed his heart, he would have ended up at the University of Southern California. "I mean the weather, the palm trees," he said. "I went out there for a visit. It was February, everything was first class, and they played the type of wide-open game that was fitting for a wide receiver. But to be honest with you, I was a momma's boy, and I didn't want to be that far away from home."

It was the late-1960s, and the Big Ten was *the* conference in White's mind. "And Ohio State was in the conference, and it was the closest Big Ten school to home at that time. During recruiting trips, I kept seeing some of the same guys at airports. We'd ask each other, 'Where are you visiting? What are you considering?' Time and again, Ohio State University was mentioned."

That sealed it for White. "We had the No. 1 or No. 2 freshman class in the nation. The talent that we had was unreal, just unreal. And then there was The Man [Hayes]. He came to my high school and spoke to the whole student body in the auditorium. I don't remember what he said specifically, but good Lord, his demeanor, his countenance. ... To play for a man like that. ... We talked about academics, and everyone knew why he was there. There were 385 in my class, and I was 42—not the brightest bulb, but hanging in there. It impressed me that he was so academically oriented."

The run to the title in 1968 added 10 victories to White's personal streak of never losing a game since his pre-junior high days. The following season, until the loss at Ann Arbor to Michigan, the streak took on eight more games. If one counts the loss his Pennsylvania all-star team took against Texas in the vaunted Big 33 Game, White endured only three defeats between the start of junior high and college graduation.

Asked to comment, he turned humble yet again. "I was just very, very fortunate," he said. "I was surrounded by so many talented athletes. I was really, really blessed."

When Hayes was recruiting White, he more was recruiting White's parents. "He was there to recruit me, but he spent almost all the time talking to my parents. I thought, "Wait! Isn't he here to recruit me?" He was very interested in my family, the kinds of friends I had, whether we went to church. My parents were hooked—I would be in the Big Ten."

In high school, White was gazelle-like. Long strides and lightning-quick speed were his hallmarks. "I was really focused on track. I enjoyed track much more than football. I didn't want to play football. Our junior high [football] coach asked me if I wanted to play. I said, 'No.' I wanted to run, and run fast, not get knocked down. 'If I get hurt playing football,' I thought, 'I can't run fast anymore.' The coach changed his approach with me, telling me football would keep me sharp for track. I was a flyer. He said, 'We're going to teach you how to soar, use your speed.' I wanted to be the fastest ever in the state of Pennsylvania."

White said he never harbored dreams of competing in track globally or even nationally. His accomplishments in high school were enough for him.

Today, he is the chief non-judicial officer of the Greene County Juvenile Court, for which he began working in January 1976.

White loves his job. "I handle everything but the judicial part," he said. "The programs for probation ... I'm responsible for budgets and grants, hiring and firing, and disciplinary problems. I enjoy it. It's a fun 'family' for me."

He and his wife, Carolyn, have three children. Their daughter Janice married recently and lives in Harrisburg; another daughter, Brandi, has an undergraduate degree in psychology and is headed for graduate school; and their son, Jamie, is at the University of Dayton.

White spends his free time by running four miles a day, playing racquetball, and doing aerobics.

"The knees are starting to ache and creak," he said, chuckling. "My days are numbered. I stay in shape as best as a 57-year-old man can."

White, who in 2000 was named to the Ohio State University All-Century Team—"It's hard to wrap my head around that," he said—is clear on how he wishes to be remembered. "As an individual who had leadership and humility, and who enjoyed the game of football at Ohio State. That would be enough for me."

17

JIM OTIS

BIRTH DATE: April 28, 1948
HOMETOWN: Celina, Ohio
RESIDENCE: St. Louis, Missouri
POSITION: Fullback
HEIGHT: 6 feet
WEIGHT: ??? pounds
YEARS: 1967 to 1969

Otis ran for more than 1,000 yards for the St. Louis Cardinals in 1975 and led the NFC in rushing. ... His father, Dr. James Otis, was a college roommate of Woody Hayes. ... His son, Jeff, played in NFL Europe this year on assignment from the now-Arizona Cardinals. ... His eldest son, Jimmy, also played for the Buckeyes.

Jim Otis is pumped after scoring another touchdown.

The Run-up

Athletes are a superstitious lot in general, prone to good-luck charms and pregame rituals they believe will help them recreate that big game they had the previous week—or month, or year.

If you ask Jim Otis, he might tell you that there is something to it. Bob Ferguson—the Buckeye fullback who epitomized Woody Hayes' grind-it-out offensive philosophy—carried OSU to the Rose Bowl with his four-touchdown, 152-yard performance against Michigan in 1961. Jim Otis was the Buckeyes' fullback on the eve of the Michigan game in 1968. An OSU victory meant a trip to the Rose Bowl.

"The night before, we had a bonfire and pep rally, where kids from the university and people from the community could come," Otis said. "Some little kid came up to me with his dad and said his dad had gotten this chin strap from Bob Ferguson after the Michigan game when he had scored four touchdowns. He wanted to give it to me, and he did.

"You could see it was pretty old and it was missing the snap, so obviously I wasn't going to wear it," he chuckled. "I thought that was pretty neat. Bob Ferguson had been a kind of hero of mine when I was a kid growing up. So I taped it on the inside of my shoulder pads, and then, the next day, I scored four touchdowns just like Bob Ferguson."

The Game
By Jim Otis

Michigan at Ohio State—November 23, 1968

We slugged it out over the first half, but we led 21-14 at the break. I'd scored two of our first three touchdowns.

I think it was Larry Zelina who made a great play, running down to the 2-yard line. It was just happenstance that Woody was standing in front of me. It was third-and-goal, and I said, "Coach, do you want that touchdown?"

He said, "Yeah, go in there and get it."

I then asked him what kind of play, and he told me, "You call the play."

I went to one of our offensive linemen, Dave Chaney, who was just a sophomore, and said, "Dave, Woody wants this coming right over you, so we better get it."

We went over the left side. I threw the ball up in the stands and chaos broke loose.

I was the kind of guy who kept the chains moving and took time off the clock, and that's what we were doing. We did that a lot at Ohio State—we outmanned people. When we got in the second half, sometimes teams would panic a bit or do things that were out of character for them.

Michigan was a lot like us. They had a great running back by the name of Ron Johnson, but they started throwing the ball. They started making mistakes—interceptions and fumbles—and we were able to score off of their mistakes. So the 50-14 score wasn't as lopsided as you would think. If you looked at the score in the book, you'd think that Ohio State really ran over them.

The Aftermath

As one might imagine, a 50-14 home win over Michigan to earn a Rose Bowl berth triggered sheer pandemonium.

"I remember all the students came out on the field," Otis said. "It was impossible to come off the field. At Ohio State, in big games, you have the crowd with you every step of the way. At professional football games, or other professional sports, you don't have the fans with you like you do at Ohio State. At other venues, the fans want to be entertained; they don't seem as interested in the game as Ohio State fans are. There are times when you can hear a pin drop, and other times the stadium is rocking. They're with you every step of the way."

The celebration was short-lived, however. After the final exams, the players shifted their focus to preparing to take on O.J. Simpson and the USC Trojans at the Rose Bowl on New Year's Day.

"Woody had us practicing at the French Fieldhouse. You talk to anybody on that team, and they won't forget this: Woody had those furnaces turned up so high that we could barely breathe. We were just wet with perspiration. Woody made sure that I never had an easy practice until I got away from Ohio State.

"It was 90 degrees the day we played the Rose Bowl, and thank God, we did all that preparation in the French Fieldhouse because we ran Southern Cal off the field that day. I don't think there was ever a team as good as the 1968-69 team. In '69, they say we walked over people, and we did—we walked over everyone."

The Michigan win, the Rose Bowl, and the '69 team were all great, but Otis said his greatest accomplishment was the work he did to get onto the field.

"When I first got [to OSU], I was way down on the list—third- or fourth-string going into spring practice. Woody had called me after spring practice and said, 'The Bucks [the offense] had scored eight times this game, and you were in on seven of those scores—I'm telling you you're going to get a chance in the fall.' I worked really hard over the summer and came back to be the starting fullback my sophomore year," Otis said proudly. "I wish every kid across the country that is a freshman or sophomore—and on the third or fourth team—would realize that almost everyone starts back in the lineup. And Woody would demote you if you weren't doing something right. It didn't matter if you were an All-American, he would demote you."

Otis' NFL career led him to St. Louis, where he and his wife of 33 years raised their children. He now works in real estate development and follows his children. His oldest daughter, Jodi, is a physical therapist and a certified trainer. The next daughter, Christine, is an obstetrician-gynecologist starting her third year of residency at the University of Virginia. His oldest son, Jimmy, played at Ohio State and is with CB Richard Ellis in Columbus in investment real estate. Their youngest son, Jeff, graduated from Columbia University, and he now plays with NFL Europe for Frankfurt Galaxy, where he was assigned by the Arizona Cardinals.

Otis wants to be remembered "... as a guy that could be relied on to do the job at hand. Whether playing on first-and-10, or fourth-and-one. Whatever my job was, my teammates knew that we would be successful. You want your teammates to believe in you 100 percent ... that there's never a doubt when you are called upon to do a task ... that when they make a great block ... that the other guy would be doing the same thing. I want to be remembered as someone who could do that—not 90 percent, but 100 percent of the time."

18

KEITH BYARS

BIRTH DATE: October 14, 1965
HOMETOWN: Dayton, Ohio
RESIDENCE: Boca Raton, Florida
POSITION: Tailback
HEIGHT: 6-foot-2
WEIGHT: 236 pounds
YEARS: 1982 to 1985

Byars was a Parade *All-American, two-time state basketball champion, and member of a state champion 4x100 relay team. ... He was named to the AFC Pro Bowl roster in 1993 while with the Miami Dolphins. ... He caught four passes and scored a touchdown in Super Bowl XXXI for the New England Patriots.*

The Run-up

Coming off a loss to Purdue, Ohio State needed a home victory against Illinois to stay in Big Ten title contention. Besides that, it was homecoming and a chance for Keith Byars to distinguish himself further.

"You always sell out the Ohio Stadium, but for this game, it seemed like they oversold it," Byars exclaimed. "They probably asked the fire marshal to look the other way. There were going to be a lot of people standing in the aisles. I always wanted to play well in the Homecoming game because it was Homecoming, and also because you could earn an extra trophy at the end of the year banquet for the MVP in the homecoming games from one of the fraternities. It was a chance to pick up some extra hardware, and I did."

The Game

By Keith Byars

Illinois at Ohio State—October 13, 1984

In the first quarter, it was Murphy's Law on the football field. Everything that could go wrong did go wrong. There were turnovers. Our defense did not tackle. Our offense did not score.

I had a fumble without being hit. I was running the ball around the left end on the sweep, and the next thing I know the ball hit my knee. Illinois recovered my fumble and scored on that drive. I knew, right then and there, that this was not going to be your typical Saturday afternoon. I had had very few fumbles in my career at Ohio State, so I thought, "For me to fumble the ball without getting hit is crazy."

When you're losing 24-0, you need someone to make a field goal; you need to get some points on the board. So when I scored the first touchdown to make the score 24-7, I had like a 16-yard touchdown run, gave someone a juke move, broke some tackles, and the next

Keith Byars, in an earlier game, eludes an Indiana defender.

thing I knew, I was in the end zone. The game was being nationally televised, so when I came onto the sidelines and looked into the cameras, along with the typical "Hi, Mom; hi, Dad, blah, blah, blah" I also said, "We're coming back!" Everyone on offense and defense felt that way after we scored. I said it, but everyone believed it. You need something good to happen. After that, it was like Murphy's Law in reverse. Everything that could go well went well.

After an Illinois fumble, Mike Tomczak found Cris Carter in double coverage in the end zone for another touchdown. Sonny Gordon grabbed an interception, and Mike Lanese caught some key passes on the ensuing drive, which set up my second touchdown of the day. The score was 24-21 at halftime.

We kind of turned the table on those guys. Instead of all the bad things happening to us, they started happening to Illinois. Going into halftime, it was a whole new ballgame. We were only down three points at the half. Just 10 minutes before, it looked bleak. Then, things looked good. You could tell how big this was going to go down in Ohio State history. People would be talking about it 30, 40, 50, 60 years after it was played.

I think Illinois fumbled the ball right after halftime, which led to my third touchdown of the day—from the 1-yard line after four consecutive carries.

I have to give credit to the offensive line—the guys up front: (Linemen) Kirk Lowdermilk, Jim Lachey, Mark Krerowicz, and (fullback) George Cooper. They were just dominating. I remember Illinois kicked off, and I caught the ball eight yards deep in the end zone. I was supposed to take the knee, but I thought, "Uh-uh, I'm bringing it out!" But I also knew I had to bring it to at least the 20-yard line, or the coaches would be all over me. So I had to break a few tackles to get it to the 24.

I was feeling real good, and that led to my infamous one-shoe football run. It was just a draw play that we ran. I remember cutting to the right and turning up field, and as soon I was getting ready to run up toward the end-zone ... I felt my shoe getting loose. So I just kicked it off and turned it into high gear. I just remember thinking, "Get to the end zone before anyone steps on your foot!" And I ran faster than I ever ran in my life. I split two defenders, and 67 yards later I had a touchdown.

My mom always told me to make sure you don't have any holes in your socks, and I didn't. I ran into the closed end of the stadium, and the fans were crazy. It was a great feeling. I felt like I was running on a cloud. I'll never forget it. I don't know how that shoe came off. The shoestring was still tied tightly after Jim Lachey handed it back to me. That was my fourth touchdown. I was so caught up in the game that I didn't realize I had four touchdowns at that time.

That game was like two heavyweight boxers going back and forth for 15 rounds, like Frazier and Ali—of course, we were Ali. We were slugging them with our best shots, and they were slugging us with their best shots. It was a knockdown, drag-out game. Whoever had the ball last would win the game.

After Illinois kicked a field goal to tie the game, as an offense, we knew we had to take over and win the football game right then—we had to score. We weren't playing for a tie; we were playing to win. We went into the two-minute offense, even though we had more than two minutes left.

The first play was a pass over the middle to Cris (Carter); which was batted down by the Illinois defender and almost intercepted. You could look at our whole offense—the linemen, the running backs— and we looked at Coach (Earle) Bruce and thought, "What is going on; why are we throwing the ball? Ohio State is a running team. We run the ball first, throw it second. So why not do what we do best? We're going to win this game by running, not by throwing an interception. If we were going to lose it, we'd lose it by doing what we do best."

So that was the last time that we threw the ball on that drive. We ran the ball 80 yards, between John Wooldridge and myself. It was a classic Ohio State drive. Woody (Hayes, Bruce's predecessor) was there at that game because it was Homecoming, so I knew that game put a big smile on his face the way we just pounded Illinois into submission. They knew we were going to run the ball; we knew we were going to run the ball; all 90,000-plus of our fans knew we were going to run the ball. And many of those watching on television knew we were going to run the ball. That is just a great feeling knowing that you're going to do something, and your opponent knows you're going to do something, but they're powerless to stop it.

The Aftermath

Of course, Byars scored the winning touchdown (his fifth of the day). Not only that, his 274 yards set a single-game record at Ohio State. All those yards caught up with Byars in the locker room.

"I was extremely tired," he said. "I was whipped, but it was a good kind of tired, knowing you did all you could. Seeing your team come together—to never quit and never die and play like that—was amazing. I've always been proud to be a Buckeye, but on that particular day, I was even more proud to wear scarlet and gray."

For Byars, much more success lay ahead. He spent more than a decade in the NFL, racking up rushing yards and catching passes for the Philadelphia Eagles, Miami Dolphins, New York Jets, and New England Patriots. Along the way, he married Margaret, and they have two kids, Taylor (14) and Keith II (11). He owns Byars Engineering and does broadcast work in Columbus, Miami, and New York.

The Illinois game was his finest performance as a Buckeye, but it's not what Byars said defined Ohio State for him.

"I'd have to say that my greatest accomplishments are the friendships that I've obtained over the years at Ohio State," Byars related. "You're 17 or 18 years old when you get there, and all the things the coaches are telling you about the friendships you'll form and your college experience sound corny. But once you get older and you look back, you realize that they were right. A lot of those guys are my best friends. Pepper Johnson and I were college roommates and have never had a cross word. We hit if off right from the beginning. Some of the best people you meet in life you met during your college years."

19

JEFF UHLENHAKE

BIRTH DATE: January 28, 1966
HOMETOWN: Newark, Ohio
RESIDENCE: Medina, Ohio
POSITION: Center
HEIGHT: 6-foot-4
WEIGHT: 250 pounds
YEARS: 1985 to 1989

A team captain, Uhlenhake participated in the protest of Coach Earle Bruce's firing in 1987. ... He switched from defensive to offensive line just prior to his (redshirt) freshman year and started all four seasons at OSU. ... He spent 10 years in the NFL, making the all-rookie team with Miami in 1989, and went on to play for New Orleans and Washington.

The Run-up

Only the hated Michigan Wolverines could have gotten the Buckeyes and their fans ready for a gloomy-day game at the end of a gloomier season.

"We really struggled my senior year," said Joe Uhlenhake. "We didn't have a very good year. It was John Cooper's first year. However, there was still a mood by the team and in the crowd to beat Michigan—it was still the Michigan game."

All that could be gained by beating Michigan at this point was a dose of satisfaction and an injection of pride. Cooper had spent much of his first season retooling the Buckeyes, which was apparent. The team lost huge to Indiana, of all teams.

"Michigan already had it wrapped up to go to the Rose Bowl that year, but we felt like we could still win and send them to the Rose Bowl on a bad note," he said. "We wanted to spoil their day and make it our day."

Uhlenhake wanted to salvage something for himself and his senior classmates in their final game at Ohio Stadium.

"After our pregame meal, the coaches left, and it was time for the seniors to speak. Normally, I was more of a quiet leader—I lead by example—but I was furious with our season. I wanted to beat Michigan so badly. So, spur of the moment, I erupted and threw a chair. I was at a boiling point, and I let loose."

The Game

By Jeff Uhlenhake

Michigan at Ohio State—November 19, 1988

Despite my speech, we were down 20-0 at halftime.

During the first half, we had a lot of three-and-outs. We weren't very productive. We could not move the ball, and Michigan kept scoring. We put our defense in bad situations on the field.

More than anything else, Jeff Uhlenhake and the Buckeyes wanted to be spoilers in this game.

The mood at halftime was depressing. I felt dejected because my so-called inspiring speech went down the drain. We shot ourselves in the foot, play after play. The younger players (juniors and sophomores)—guys like Jeff Davidson, Joe Staysniak, Bo Pelini, and Jimmy Peel—were the ones to pick us up. They told us they were going to help, and they were going to send the seniors out on a good note. During halftime, the seniors weren't as vocal as we were before the game—particularly me.

The second half brought forth more of a statement from the sluggish Buckeyes.

The seniors and underclassmen fought like hell in the second half. After halftime, I went back out feeling like, "This is Michigan. It's 20-0, and we're not going to embarrass ourselves." And we didn't. Even though we lost, we played admirably well.

They couldn't stop the running game—Bill Matlock, Jaymes Bryant, and Carlos Snow—and we racked up 469 total offensive yards.

How often do you see that in a Michigan game? Usually it's a defensive battle. It was a very tight game. We had one key series where we had to settle for a field goal. We had a chance to get our fourth touchdown and couldn't get it. That probably was the difference in the game.

I thought it was a sterling second half ... we fought our asses off until the very end. I can look back with pride, because I knew it was such a valiant effort.

The Aftermath

No matter how valiant the effort, a loss at the end of a lost season was tough to take.

"We were disappointed with the game," Uhlenhake admitted. "There were hugs all around. People wanted to console you because you just lost to Michigan. Everyone was saying they enjoyed playing with you. We all knew a period in our lives was over. We knew we wouldn't be around each other much in the future. Usually, you have bowl practices and a bowl game to look forward to, so we were all dejected—especially the seniors—sitting in front of our lockers, knowing it was all over. You always wanted to beat Michigan."

It was the first of 10 losses to Michigan by Cooper-coached teams, compared to two victories and a tie. Sadly, that became the catalyst in the coach's termination.

"Uhly", as his teammates know him, will always remember that game as the hallmark of his college career.

"It's all about doing well and beating Michigan, because you're always judged by beating Michigan. And although we didn't, we left the field knowing we did our best coming back from that deficit—and I did it with some of my best friends for life."

Uhlenhake graduated from Ohio State University in 1989 and went on to 10 good years in the NFL. He is now married to Angie, and the happy couple had their first child in the summer of 2006. He is now an assistant offensive line coach for the Cleveland Browns, working under offensive line coach (and ex-Buckeye) Jeff Davidson.

20

JERRY RUDZINSKI

BIRTH DATE: July 16, 1975
HOMETOWN: Centerville, Ohio
RESIDENCE: Columbus, Ohio
POSITION: Linebacker
HEIGHT: 6-foot-1
WEIGHT: 220 pounds
YEARS: 1995 to 1998

He was Defensive Player of the Year for the State of Ohio, two-time first-team All-State, and MVP for the Greater Catholic League while at Kettering (Ohio) Alter High School.

Jerry Rudzinski recalls the Buckeyes overcoming adversity.

The Run-up

You've heard the cliché: This one was for all the marbles.

"It was an emotional Senior Day," Rudzinski explained. "We knew the Big Ten Championship was on the line. We knew this would be our last time in Ohio Stadium. We knew we had to beat Michigan. It was tiring because of the mental preparation. Before every pregame, our coaches, managers, and trainers would leave the locker room. Just the senior players would speak. On this particular occasion, we were in the locker room longer, though we spoke fewer words. It was a bigger message, but less was said. The senior captains told the rest of the team, 'If you're a perimeter player, play with finesse, and make the plays that are needed. If you're not a perimeter player, go get in a fist fight.'"

The Buckeyes had cruised through most of the year ranked No. 1 but fell late in the Big Ten season after a heartbreaking 28-24 loss to Michigan State.

"After Michigan State, the seniors pulled together and said we could do two things: We could go through the motions and roll our helmets, and with our talented team, we would probably still do well; or we could focus our talent and determination and finish what we started," he remembered. "We decided to finish what we started. So we got better against Iowa and were determined not to let Michigan beat us. We ended up No. 2 in the polls and had fought back from adversity.

"When we came out of the locker room, the seniors saw our parents at the end of the tunnel of pride. We lingered for a moment. Seeing my parents was the most emotional moment of my college career. My parents and I had tears of happiness in our eyes. They had helped me so much from Day One. It was one of the greatest days of my life and of their lives."

The Game

By Jerry Rudzinski

Michigan at Ohio State—November 21, 1998

Our top priority was to keep Michigan quarterback Tom Brady from controlling the ball and, therefore, the clock. It was his last game, too, and we knew our defense would have to show up and play for all four quarters. We knew we could not completely stop Tom, but our goal was to slow him down. We were very successful. We held their rushing game to under 10 yards.

We soon settled in, and the offense made some big plays. (Tailback) Michael Wiley ripped off a 53-yard run that stunned Michigan, and Dee Miller got a touchdown catch soon thereafter. David Boston caught two more touchdown passes from Joe (Germaine), and we had a 21-10 lead at the half.

Antoine Winfield put on some of the biggest plays of his life. He was only 170 pounds and played like he was 270 pounds. During the third quarter I made an interception. I tipped the ball and kept it alive. It was an amazing feeling to take a ball away from Tom Brady. Coach (Fred) Pagac (the assistant head coach that also handled the linebackers) said a great athlete would have caught that and run it into the end zone—and then he bear hugged me and wrestled me to the ground. While I've had better games personally, this was more of a team game.

We were successful because we each just did our own job. Sometimes in other games, we would have a breakdown trying to help each other, say when our players would try to do two players' or three players' jobs instead of just focusing on their own. However, this game was one of our best defensive performances as a team.

The Aftermath

There is no party like a post-Michigan victory party at Ohio State.

"I knew the crowd would rush the field like they had the last time we beat Michigan. It was like a party with 95,000 people," Rudzinski said. "Every Ohio State fan was slapping shoulder pads, helmets, trying to lift us up on their shoulders. I wasn't in any hurry to get in the locker room. I wanted to savor the moment. When I finally made it into the locker room, I found out that I was the last player in—the team was waiting on me to sing the fight song. I've never heard it sung so loud and so personal. I've never seen so many happy football players in my life. It was a time where the players wanted to be with one another. No one was in a hurry to leave; we didn't want to take off our shoulder pads. Cooper had a lot of comments for the seniors. He knew our ups and our downs. There's nothing better than beating Michigan during your senior year at a home game."

Team accomplishments are what Rudzinski takes the most pride in.

"My greatest accomplishment would be leaving Ohio State with 43 wins after four years of eligibility," he said. "We left there with the winningest class in Ohio State history. As a fan of OSU football, this meant the world to me. I was captain of a group of players that I not only liked, but looked up to and admired."

The intervening years have been just as good to Rudzinski. Now the regional manager for Stryker Corporation in Columbus, he also broadcasts football for 1460-The Fan (WBNS-AM). He's married to Marcia, and they have a son and a daughter. To scratch that competitive itch, Rudzinski has run three half-marathons, one full marathon, and a half-Ironman triathlon.

21

WILLIAM WHITE

BIRTH DATE: February 19, 1966
HOMETOWN: Lima, Ohio
RESIDENCE: Powell, Ohio
HEIGHT: 5-foot-10
WEIGHT: 205 pounds
POSITION: Defensive back
YEARS: 1984 to 1987

William was selected by the Detroit Lions in the fourth round (85th pick overall) of the 1988 NFL Draft. ... Was the Lions' 1992 Edge NFL Man of the Year. ...Traded by the Detroit Lions to the Kansas City Chiefs for a 1995 conditional draft pick on July 13, 1994. ... Registered 178 career tackles at Ohio State, where he earned a degree in metallurgical engineering. ... The first-team All-Big Ten selection also grabbed 16 interceptions and scored two touchdowns over his four years with the Buckeyes. ... Attended OSU during the off-seasons to fulfill his degree requirements. ... Ran for 1,444 yards as a two-way performer at Lima High School. ... Academic All-Big Ten in 1986 and 1987, during which he received the Best Student Athlete and Arnie Chonko awards. ... In 1987, he was selected as the Cotton Bowl Scholar Athlete. ... When he graduated from OSU, he received the prestigious Dr. St. Pierre Award from the Metallurgical Department. ... He took the field as a starter at the strong safety position in the 1999 Super Bowl with the Atlanta Falcons, leading the team on defense with nine tackles.

The Run-up

William White remembers a packed, loud house when Ohio State encountered the host Wolverines on a sun-splashed Saturday afternoon.

"It was typical of the OSU-Michigan game," White said. "Standing room only, even though it was not as important to them as it was to us."

It may have been boisterous in Michigan Stadium that day, but White and his fellow Buckeyes were playing with decidedly heavy hearts. The university had dispatched their coach, Earle Bruce, the previous Monday. Images of Bruce standing in tears on his lawn—with members of the OSU marching band on hand playing the Buckeye Battle Cry—would be etched indelibly on the memories of anyone who was a Buckeye fan or had a television. Bruce was fired for having the audacity to average a mere nine victories per year. Nine-and-three wouldn't cut it. The decision didn't cut it with his charges, though, either. They were feeling betrayed, bewildered, and completely let down.

A co-captain in his senior year, this game was an overly emotional affair—not just for White, but also for his fellow seniors.

"It was hard on the four of us senior co-captains—[linebacker Chris] Spielman, [linebacker Eric] Kumerow, [quarterback-punter Tom] Tupa and me—when we realized that Coach Bruce had been fired, and that we would be deprived of a bowl game as seniors. We were outraged," White related. "The first couple of practices that week were depressing. Everyone was down. The four of us co-captains went in to see [then-President Edward] Jennings to speak our minds. Even though we knew Jennings probably wouldn't change his mind, we needed to get this off our chests. We felt like he didn't understand the impact on us. On Thursday, our practices started getting better. On Friday, I flunked my engineering 501 exam—the only exam I ever flunked at Ohio State. I was that upset. [Later] on Friday, we went to Michigan. [Offensive lineman Joe] Staysniak came up the idea to wear headbands with Earle's name on them. I don't remember the pregame

William White gets ready to lower the boom on an opponent.

speech, but all along Coach Bruce was a class act. He reminded us that the game was not about him. He said the game was why we came to OSU."

No one could keep the Buckeyes from getting the last word, though. They had a steely determination about them. As they took the field for pregame warmups, it was a focused bunch—with a massive chip on its shoulder.

The Game

By William White

Ohio State at Michigan—November 21, 1987

Just before the kickoff, while standing on the sidelines, Bruce turned around to see every member of the team take off his helmet. Each wore a white headband with the word EARLE written on it in black marker.

While I personally had better games, the reason this was the game of my life was because my teammates rallied together for a common goal. This was what the game of football was all about. Our team wasn't one of the best teams that OSU had put on the field. We had a young offense; most of our experience was on the defense. Both Spielman and I were four-year starters.

Michigan had a good first half. We were still feeling sorry for ourselves. We felt the impact that this was our last game as seniors. Michigan's running back had 110 yards rushing in the first half alone. Michigan came out the second half thinking they could run the ball.

The first-half huddles were solemn. We were going through the motions. At halftime, in the locker room, Spielman went off. He rallied the team and told us to do a gut check. We left the locker room energized. We knew we had to play the second half with passion. The game plan didn't change, but our attitude did. It was like all of those clichés: 'never give up,' 'stay the course,' etc. Michigan won the first half; we owned the second. (Defensive back) Greg Rogan came out and deflected a pass. (Defensive back) David Brown also had a big hit. I hit someone for a two- to three-yard loss on third-and-1. All these plays contributed to our 23-20 win.

The Aftermath

In the end, the Buckeyes delivered their intended message for their coach and the outgoing seniors. A victory in the Big House by any team is a monumental achievement; that Ohio State pulled it off under such adverse circumstances was even more amazing.

The sense of accomplishment was overwhelming, considering the attendant circumstances, still White remembers feeling "great."

"We knew we had come together as a team for our coach," he explained. "It was very satisfying as a senior, especially since we weren't going to a bowl game."

And just like that—in a blink of an eye—the season, the seniors' careers, and the coach's employment were history. There was very little fanfare in Columbus, no huge crowds awaiting the Buckeyes' charter flight back from Michigan; the opposite often was the case. White and his teammates had made good on their intention to send the senior class and the coach out as winners, though, and that was good enough for White. He said he considers this victory and his graduation from the university as his greatest accomplishments.

The trip down U.S. 23—really, High Street extended—to go to Ohio State seemed a natural route to White.

"Being an Ohio boy, I always wanted to go to OSU," White said. "As accolades started coming in from all over the country, I thought I'd at least go visit other places—just because. When I came to visit OSU, they took us to Ohio Union. [Bruce's predecessor as coach] Woody Hayes was on hand and came up to my parents and me. He welcomed me but then turned his back to me to talk to my parents the whole time.

"I was thinking, 'Hey, *I'm the man*; you shouldn't be talking to my parents, but to me.' Of course, Woody knew what he was doing. After he left, my Dad said, 'You are going to Ohio State.' So, I really had no choice at that point. Besides, I had Cris Carter, who already knew he was going to OSU, telling me, 'If you don't come to OSU, I'll be beating up on you wherever you are, so you might as well play for OSU.'"

White was active in sports from an early age. By the time he arrived at Lima Senior High School, he was ready for anything. He achieved tons, earning all-Miami Conference, all-Lima, and All-State in football. He also was a basketball player for the Spartans.

These days, White is a church developer. "I design, oversee, and secure funding for the development of churches for SRP Development," he said. "I have been married to the most wonderful lady, Nikol, for 10 years. I have a 22-year-old, William; a seven-year-old, Brendan; and a five-year-old, Brea, whose birthday party I have to rush off to right now."

He said he thoroughly enjoys his family time and playing golf when he can get some free time.

Dependability in life is what White relishes—his and that of others.

"I would like to be remembered as having my teammates and coaches being able to count on me," White said. "I'd like to be known for having been dependable, trustworthy, and that my teammates knew that I would be where they wanted me to be. Knowing that my teammates respected me enough to be voted co-captain was my reward for what I brought to the team."

During his induction ceremony to the Lima Senior High School Hall of Fame, White said, "Everything starts with your attitude. Your attitude is the beginning of who you're going to be."

That's precisely what White tells young people when he delivers motivational talks at schools, and this is what has led him, from an early age, to his own achievements.

22

DIMITRIOUS STANLEY

BIRTH DATE: September 19, 1974
HOMETOWN: Worthington, Ohio
RESIDENCE: Columbus, Ohio
POSITION: Wide Receiver
HEIGHT: 5-foot-10
WEIGHT: 181 pounds
YEARS: 1993 to 1997

Played with the Miami Dolphins and Winnipeg Blue Bombers. ... Gave his Rose Bowl ring to his father. ... He was a keynote speaker at an America's Promise event in Columbus to "keep the lights on after school."

The Run-up

Unknown to Dimitrious Stanley's teammates (and to himself, probably), his "psychic" ability would manifest itself in the Rose Bowl, in front of 105,000 fans and millions more across the country. Later, the same phenomenon manifested itself against future Denver Broncos quarterback Jake "the Snake" Plummer and linebacker Pat Tillman, who later would die an American hero in the hills of Afghanistan as a result of friendly fire in the war against terror.

"The day before the game, I walked the field with [defensive lineman] Matt Finkes," Stanley explained. "We went down to our end zone, and I told him that I would score right there. When I scored my long touchdown, it was right in that exact spot."

The 1997 game would be the first and only trip to the Rose Bowl for Stanley and his classmates.

"Our 1993 class included some special players such as Shawn Springs and Anthony Gwinn," he said. "You could tell it in everyone's eyes that we knew how special our opportunity to play in the Rose Bowl was. You could tell it by the way everyone hugged each other. Nothing was said, but we knew. Everyone was in their own little world."

The Game

By Dimitrious Stanley

Ohio State vs. Arizona State
The Rose Bowl—January 1, 1997

I told our quarterbacks coach, Walt Harris, that if the ball were thrown to me across the middle, I'd score. We had a 15-yard big return for a first down, then Joey Galloway threw a post route across the middle to me, and I ran it in for a 72-yard touchdown.

No one expected a 72-yard touchdown from me. It was the longest Rose Bowl play for 10 years. It was especially significant for me because no one expected such a play from me. I didn't run a 4.3-second 40-yard dash like Joey Galloway or Terry Glenn, so not only did I have a big play, but I had it in the Rose Bowl.

It was also gratifying to burn the defensive back who had been trying to get in my head all game.

Arizona State's No. 22 was a little guy who had been talking crap to me. He thought he was playing great defense, but we had been playing the same plays, so it wasn't really due to any smarts on his part. He'd bump me on the shoulder, and I'd just look at him.

I told him, "Alright, dude, you're not playing good defense." Then I had my big play, and it was clear that I was the victor. Once you get guys like that talking back, you get them off track. They're no longer focused on the game—they're focused on you. They forget that there are 10 other people on the field.

We were down 17-13 in the last two minutes, and Arizona State was closing in on a national title.

There was 1:19 left in the game, and we were down. … I helped get three first downs and had one pass-interference play, as did David Boston, which got us down to around the 7-yard line. On the last play, I was on the inside, and Dave was on the outside in a twin set. I ran up the corner, curling up in the middle to hold the defenders on me. They quadruple-teamed me, leaving Dave open. This gave Dave room to score the winning touchdown.

The Aftermath

The 20-17 victory was sweet, but not only because it cemented Ohio State's No. 2 ranking that year and gave Stanley, Glenn, and Springs a Rose Bowl win. It also became coach John Cooper's first Rose Bowl victory since defeating Michigan as the coach of— ironically enough—Arizona State.

"I said before the game that if we won, I was going to sit in the middle of the field," Stanley said. "So that's what I did, and the rest of the team ran out to join me. While sitting there, I watched my team

Dimitrious Stanley and The Best Damned Band in the Land celebrate his 72-yard score.

celebrate and watched the reaction of the crowd. I wanted to be on the outside looking in. I reflected on my memories of my dad's coaching career at OSU. As a coach, my father didn't win the Rose Bowl, so it had a different meaning for me. I remembered that when I was a kid I used to play with these Rose Bowl and Fiesta Bowl emblems, which I would stick on my shirt. And there, I was being a part of a team that just won the Rose Bowl."

What was Stanley's greatest achievement at Ohio State? Was it the Rose Bowl win?

"No, being a starting receiver was a greater accomplishment. My coach did not believe I would start," he admitted. "I wasn't the typical physical wide receiver. I was more mental and approached catching the ball more as a science. Having my coach and others say I couldn't do it made me excel. It wasn't obvious that I could be as good as I was until they put me in the game because I wasn't the fastest or strongest."

When Stanley, a bachelor, isn't working his day job, he plays golf, mixes music, and gives back to the community.

"I'm selling flooring to builders for Custom Flooring Distributors, a sister company of Rite Rug," he said. "I also started Camp Mind Games for nine-to-13-year-olds. The camp allows kids to participate in art, reading, computers, football, basketball, and golf. We try to use physical activities to engage their minds. I also do public speaking to juvenile detention centers and at OSU alumni events."

23

DEE MILLER

BIRTH DATE: December 4, 1975
HOMETOWN: Springfield, Ohio
RESIDENCE: Pataskala, Ohio
POSITION: Flanker
HEIGHT: 6-foot-1
WEIGHT: 200 pounds
YEARS: 1995 to 1998

Miller was a two-sport star for Springfield South High School, where he played football and basketball. In football, he was an All-American, a Parade All-American, and Ohio's High School Player of the Year. The Green Bay Packers chose him in the sixth round of the 1999 draft.

144

The Run-up

Dee Miller got exactly what he expected for the annual showdown with Michigan, this one in Ohio Stadium: decent weather and a boisterous assemblage of Buckeye faithful.

"It was pretty good for November; the sun was shining," Miller said. "The crowd was very rowdy, but that's to be expected against Michigan."

The game represented the OSU departure point for a virtual "Who's Who" of Buckeye players.

"It was very intense," he said. "It was my senior year with Damon Moore, Antoine Winfield, Joe Germaine, Joe Montgomery, David Boston, and Andy Katzenmoyer. It was emotional because we knew it was our last game. We were excited and looked forward to the game.

"I was heavily recruited by Michigan. Jim Herrmann, the defensive coordinator for Michigan who recruited me, would always look at me [from] the 50-yard line. Every Michigan game, we walked through the Tunnel of Pride—where all the former players would line up—and we would run through the tunnel. Many of us got teary-eyed running out of the Tunnel of Pride, because we were trying to *not* lose our last game against Michigan at home. It was great to go out on a winning note."

The Buckeyes fairly punished Michigan, 31-19. In this series, the score represented a blowout.

"It was the competition, the meaning behind the rivalry," Miller said. "During my tenure, we were 2-3 against Michigan. I scored a touchdown during that game. It was the game of my life because we won in Ohio Stadium, on my last game, and in front of my family and friends."

Miller was able to get the last word as well.

"One of my best friends, Marcus Ray, was a Michigan safety; and he played on my side of the field," Miller said. "For years before this, Marcus talked a lot of trash to me. I always gave him a wink when I walked by him. During my freshman year against Michigan, we won, but I was red-shirted. My junior year, I was starting, but we didn't win.

Dee Miller heads downfield against Indiana earlier in the season.

So for my senior year, it was all for keeps. It felt like it was my team, my game.

"There was still the usual trash talking," Miller continued. "We'd been hearing the same comments for years. We were on the talking side, too. The media had misconstrued comments by one or two of our players, and things got a bit heated. We advised everyone to play it cool because we didn't want to give anyone any ammunition."

The Game

By Dee Miller

Michigan at Ohio State—November 21, 1998

On the drive on which I scored, we had a strong running game in place with Joe Montgomery, Michael Wiley, and the downfield blocking of wide receiver David Boston. We made it to their 20-yard line. I ran a post route, and Andre Weathers was covering me. Marcus was a safety on my side. Unfortunately for Marcus, he fell for the fake run by Joe Germaine.

Joe looked to run; Marcus took off after Joe, thinking he was going to make a tackle. Once he realized Joe was tossing it, he jumped but not high enough to catch it. He might have tipped it. I ran behind Marcus to make the catch in the end zone.

Afterwards, I strutted up to the sideline and pointed up to my mom.

The Aftermath

Miller said his greatest game brought him liberation.

"I was relieved because I didn't want to lose to Michigan, especially my senior year," he said. "I wanted to win for my teammates—guys like Germaine, Boston, Winfield, who would go on to the pros. I wanted to win for our fans, and I knew Coach [John] Cooper needed a win. It was also bittersweet because it was my last game at OSU, but, unlike a couple of previous classes, we went out winning."

Miller said helping the Buckeyes beat Michigan wasn't his greatest success off the field. "I'd say representing the university well, never getting in trouble, and coming back and getting my degree in 2001 would be my greatest accomplishments," he said.

Miller ended up at OSU because his parents wanted to see him go there.

"I wanted to go to Tennessee and play with Peyton Manning, who would have been in my same class," Miller said. "I was a mama's boy, an only child, and wanted to go to the NFL. However, my parents stressed the importance of being loyal to the state of Ohio. In hindsight, I'm glad they were persuasive."

Today, Miller still is taking care of business, albeit of a different sort.

"I've owned a State Farm [insurance] agency in Hilliard since January of this year," he said. "I love being part of Hilliard and being 30 minutes from my hometown."

Miller's parents "… still live in Springfield with my four-year-old brother. I married my wife, Lisa, in August 2005. I like hanging out with my family. I'm active in local civic organizations, too. I enjoy giving some time back. I speak to different youth organizations, schools, and juvenile-detention facilities."

Miller asks fans to remember him "… as someone who came in and worked hard to be the best he could be—as someone with great hands, who arrived as a good football player, and left there as part of one of the best teams at Ohio State."

24

BILL LONG

BIRTH DATE: June 4, 1947
HOMETOWN: West Milton, Ohio
RESIDENCE: Columbus, Ohio
POSITION: Quarterback
HEIGHT: 6-foot-2
WEIGHT: 185 pounds
YEARS: 1966 to 1968

Long went to Milton-Union and Stebbins high schools in west-central Ohio. ... Played football, basketball and baseball. ... Was All-Ohio in baseball and honorable mention in football. ... Ended up at Ohio State, "... Because my ass is painted Scarlet and Gray, as my dad would say. But in the end, truthfully, Woody gets you. How can you say no to the SOB? My family and I went to see an OSU basketball game on a recruiting trip. At halftime, Woody took me up to his office in St. John Arena. We didn't talk football. He pulled one of his favorite books, Words with Power out of his desk and began to grill me. 'Spell establishment. Define it. Use it in a sentence.' After that, he said to me, 'Bill, why don't we just get this thing over with? Commit now.' Well, we went back downstairs, found my parents, Bob and Shorty, and went out to dinner. Ritter Collet, the sports editor of the Dayton Daily News was there, and Woody said to him, 'Ritter, Bill has something to tell you.' And like an idiot, I said I'd committed to OSU—and there went the rest of my trips!"

The Run-up

Bill Long feels that one shouldn't consider statistics as the primary factor when determining the greatest game of an athlete's career, stating that many elements surrounding a game should be taken into account, including strength of opposition, the significant elements of the game itself, and even the timing of the game. An unranked, non-conference game early in the season means very little, Long says, compared to say a Big Ten-championship game against Michigan at the end of the year. Some might also suggest that the result of the actual contest be considered, i.e., should one's achievements in a losing effort equal those in a victory?

"In my three-year span with the Buckeyes [freshmen were not eligible in my era], I had the privilege to play a part in what I'd consider four great games: against Michigan State in 1966, against Purdue in 1968, against Michigan in 1968, and the 1969 Rose Bowl game against O.J. Simpson's Southern Cal Trojans.

"Unfortunately my role in three of these games was of a minor nature, although it is true my only play against Purdue is considered somewhat significant. This leaves the '66 Michigan State game as the game of my life.

"It was only my fourth start at QB, and the Michigan State team was ranked No.1 in the nation, and even more significant is they were considered one of the best teams in the history of college football. You might remember, this was the team that played to the historic 10-10 tie with Notre Dame later that same year. After Michigan State demolished us up in East Lansing the year before, I clearly remember what our then-starting quarterback, Don Unverferth, said to me at practice:

"'Be ready next year for George Webster, Long.' He wasn't smiling when he said it."

In '65, OSU wasn't merely beaten, "We were beaten up," Long says. On the '65 and '66 teams, MSU had All-Americans: linebacker George Webster, defensive end Bubba Smith, and wide receiver Gene Washington.

Bill Long is perhaps better known for his decisive touchdown against Purdue in 1968.

The Game

By Bill Long

Michigan State at Ohio State—November 17, 1967

The elements would play a significant role in this contest. A windy, torrential rain started before the game and lasted all afternoon. Assistant coach Floyd Stahl said it was the worst conditions ever faced at the stadium except for the 1950 Snow Bowl against Michigan. The rain was so bad that both teams warmed up outside the stadium, and neither band marched at halftime. We were a three-touchdown underdog.

Our defense played brilliantly, and we led 2-0 at the half. MSU's barefoot kicker, Dick Kenney, made a field goal in the third quarter.

On the first play of the fourth quarter Woody called 'Anders', which was an isolation pass to Billy Ray that we put into our arsenal just for this game. I hit him in stride for a 47-yard touchdown. Again, like it happened in the '67 Illinois game, Michigan State drove the length of the field to score a fourth-down, controversial TD to win the game, 11-8.

Unfortunately for me, history only remembers winners.

The Aftermath

In the 1968 season, Long, subbing at quarterback one play for an injured Rex Kern, actually scored the deciding touchdown in a 13-0 victory against Purdue, derailing Purdue's reign on No. 1 and knocking the Boilermakers from Rose Bowl contention. That OSU team went on to beat Southern Cal 27-16 in the Rose Bowl for the national championship.

Long graduated from Ohio State University in 1970 with a degree in fine arts. After attempting a career in professional sports, he enrolled in law school, where the political bug bit him. That bite lured him into a 25-year lobbying career.

These days, he teaches part-time, rescues stray animals all the time, and lobbies on behalf of animal welfare organizations. Presently, he is working on two new books, a second novel and a non-fiction sports book. Mr. Long's first book was a semi-autobiographical novel titled *Black Bridge*.

His was an idyllic childhood, Long said. "We were a close-knit family in a small Midwestern town of about 2,500 people. My dad was the football coach, so I grew up around sports and played them the whole time. Sport was the center of everything. It was a wonderful existence."

He has a grown daughter and two sisters, the younger of which was born on November 18, 1967—the day Long threw and ran for touchdowns in a 21-10 victory against Iowa.

25

BOB BRUDZINSKI

BIRTH DATE: January 1, 1955
HOMETOWN: Fremont, Ohio
RESIDENCE: Fort Lauderdale, Florida
POSITION: Defensive end
HEIGHT: 6-foot-4
WEIGHT: 228 pounds
YEARS: 1973 to 1976

Let Brudzinski tell it, tongue firmly planted in cheek: "In high school, I was All-Everything: All-State, All-County, All-District, Lineman of the Year for the state of Ohio, North-South Ohio All-Star Game, and the Big 33, where Ohio plays against Pennsylvania," he said. ... He also played basketball and baseball. "I probably could have played [basketball] for a small college," he said. Instead, he was a first-round draft pick by the Los Angeles Rams, where he played for four years and continued in the NFL for nine more years with the Miami Dolphins.

The Run-up

Bob Brudzinski loved this football Saturday. For one thing, the game was at Ann Arbor, Michigan—and it's always nice to go to your archrival's place and kick some butt.

"It was the same crummy, old Michigan weather," Brudzinksi muttered. "Overcast. Crummy turf. It was like playing on asphalt. The crowd, [approximately] 100,000 people, was definitely loud. ... We were both undefeated going into that game.

"We were number one in the country at that time. There was a lot of hoopla for that game. Woody [Hayes] brought the defense into his office at St. John Arena [on the OSU campus]. He put us together and had us interlock our arms. He got in the middle and tried to break free from us. He couldn't get out. He told us that's how he wanted us to play the next day as a team—no holes. Woody was a great motivator and speaker."

The Game

By Bob Brudzinski

Ohio State at Michigan—November 22, 1975

On the day of the game, we felt a lot of nervousness, but we were psyched. Assistant coach Esco Sarkkinen, who had been All-America in 1939, stood on the sideline, and, right before the game, he put his arm around me and told me I was one of the best players he had ever coached. That meant the world to me. He had been the best teacher, the best coach I've ever had. What he taught me stayed with me throughout my career.

Coach Hayes always had the loud speakers going to get us used to how loud the crowd was for Michigan games. It was crowd noise the whole time. You end up getting a headache after practice. I always wondered what the students thought. We always did the same Senior

In a tune-up for the Michigan game, Bob Brudzinski returns a Purdue turnover.

Tackle stuff, and we might have had more press out there because it was Archie Griffin's last game.

To beat Michigan is the best—to get the gold pants (a gold charm on a necklace that represents a victory against Michigan). My freshman year, I broke my thumb and had to watch the game from the stands, so this was my first time to actually play in Michigan Stadium.

The locker rooms were really crummy, which was typical of visitors' locker rooms. I'm sure Woody gave one of his great pregame speeches. I remember coming out of that real long tunnel that goes down on an angle on that field, because that field is dug down into the ground. We were very psyched for that game.

It was also pretty cool to play against one of my high school teammates, Rob Lytle, a tailback-fullback, who later played for the Denver Broncos of the NFL. Beating them gave me bragging rights. When you play against someone you know, you just want to give it a little extra pop when you hit them. It just feels good. It feels good because you know you didn't let him get away. When I tackled him, I'd say hi to him—nothing mean-spirited.

It was a great game—a 21-14 victory. Everyone played well. I had a good game all along, but towards the end, I had a part in two critical plays that helped turn the momentum and helped us win the game.

During a critical drive in the fourth quarter, I was in on a sack of Michigan's quarterback Rick Leach for a nine-yard loss. The score was tied at the time. The next play, it was third-and-long, I got back in deep pass coverage, what was called "Cover 2," and I had a good drop, so he had to lob it over me. It had too much arc on it. I almost touched it, but by lobbing it over me, it gave our defensive back, Ray Griffin, a chance to react. He was able to intercept it and took it down to the 3-yard line. Pete Johnson ended up scoring off of that. It was a big momentum shift.

The Aftermath

The "crummy" locker room was the site of great celebration, a happy Brudzinski reports.

"[Later that night, once back in Columbus], they let the whole team get on *The Woody Hayes Show*. That was pretty funny. Looking back we look pretty funny, too, the way we dressed. Timmy Fox had long hair and sunglasses. [Nick] Buonamici had an all-leather outfit on and earrings and curly hair and hat. Oh, God, the plaids that we wore back then. Woody tried to ask us questions on the show, but then he'd answer them for us. He'd say something like, 'Isn't that right, son?' And then he would answer the question himself. We didn't say much unless he asked us about school or our parents. Woody was like a father figure to us. Playing for Ohio State was like being in a fraternity. I don't think any of us joined a fraternity because we had each other."

What was Brudzinski's greatest accomplishment as a Buckeye?

"It was the pride of being able to play for Coach Hayes and in Ohio Stadium and playing with great guys," he said. "Even in the pros, when we saw someone who played for Ohio State, we always talked to them because we were part of something special. Even nowadays, when I see someone like Keith Byars, Cris Carter, or Paul Warfield down here in Florida, it's just a neat feeling."

That he ended up playing college football for a major program with a rabid following may be considered a bit surprising.

"I didn't watch college ball," admitted Brudzinski. "There wasn't much on TV at the time. I made three school visits in high school to OSU, Michigan, and Michigan State. I didn't have time to make any other visits because I was busy playing basketball. When I visited Michigan State, it snowed like three feet that day. [MSU coach] Denny Stoltz was put on probation that year for illegal recruiting. My freshman class there would have been placed on probation. I thought Bo [Schembechler, former Michigan coach and Hayes protégé] was great, but I did not care for the school. [OSU safety] Craig Cassady took me around OSU. I had a great visit. It didn't hurt that my dad wanted me to go there. In fact, he probably would have disowned me if I hadn't."

Brudzinski was reared in Fremont, Ohio. "My dad worked in a factory and my mom also worked. I was lucky enough to play football. I probably would not have gone to college without the scholarship."

These days, Brudzinski is in business himself as the owner of five restaurants in Palm Beach and Broward counties in Florida, called Bru's Room Sports Grill. "I met my partner after one of the [Miami] Dolphins' games tailgating. He told me one day he was going to get me into the restaurant business."

He also is the father of two boys. "One is studying hotel-restaurant management at the University of Central Florida; he had a football scholarship at the University of Massachusetts. My youngest is a red-shirt freshman at the University of Toledo. Both of them are linebackers."

Naturally.

Brudzinski, who is able to golf year-round in South Florida, said he also enjoys skiing trips, hunting, and cycling. He said he would like to be remembered "… as being consistent on the field. One of Woody Hayes' sayings was that everyone makes mistake, but you learn from your mistakes. I tried very hard not to make the same mistake twice. If a guy burned me once, I wouldn't let it happen again. I wasn't a flashy player, nor was I a vocal leader. I tried to lead by example. It's the same as in business; if I work hard by jumping in and being hands-on instead of sitting, watching, and telling people what to do, then hopefully my employees will see that this guy isn't afraid to get his hands dirty and do what it takes to be successful."

26

CHARLIE REAM

BIRTH DATE: December 12, 1913
HOMETOWN: Navarre, Ohio
RESIDENCE: Bexley, Ohio
POSITION: Tackle-tight end
HEIGHT: 6-foot-2
WEIGHT: 228 pounds
YEARS: 1935 to 1937

Ream was a walk-on at Ohio State. ... Played two years for the Cleveland Rams, before they became the Los Angeles and finally the St. Louis Rams. ... Was a physical conditioning instructor at the Iowa City Pre-Flight School for the U.S. Navy, for which he became one of the few, if not the only, former Buckeyes to have played against his alma mater. ... Had two Navy teammates with the Seahawks, Jim Langhurst and Dick Fisher, who later played with the Ohio State football team.

The Run-up

The fans didn't care about all the late fall rain—more than 80,000 showed up to watch Charlie Ream and the Buckeyes take on Notre Dame, the No. 1 team in the country, for the national championship.

"Back then, playing Michigan wasn't that big of a deal. We had beaten them three years in a row and held them scoreless," Ream said. "The Notre Dame game, however, was different. They were undefeated, and we had never played them before. Also, this was during the Depression. People living during that time didn't have much to get excited about. Most were out of jobs, and everyone was pretty down in the dumps. However, it seemed like everyone looked forward to this game."

Ream, like many other Catholic kids, was a Fighting Irish fan growing up. Now in his 90s, he reminisced fondly.

"Knute Rockne had established this incredible tradition at Notre Dame, and, in fact, I had wanted to play there," he said. "But being part of this great matchup during such a difficult time and being able to cheer folks up for a bit was a wonderful experience for a young fellow from a small town in Ohio.

"It was quiet in the locker room," Ream remembered. "We always had a blackboard meeting. My coach, Francis Schmidt, had come to us from a Christian school; yet, he could really swear. He told us, 'We're going to go out and beat those *so-and-so* Irish boys.' My other coach, Ernie Godfrey, was very religious. He was quiet and would not dream of swearing.

"There were a lot parties around campus before the game, especially in the fraternity and sorority houses, and it seemed like every sportswriter around the country was coming to this game.

"At that time, they gave sophomores two free tickets to the game. I took my two tickets [face value $3.75 each] to my fraternity house, the Betas, and sold them for $25 each to fraternity brothers. I had $50 in my pocket and felt like a millionaire. Those guys probably turned around and sold them for even more money. You could not get tickets

Back in 1935, Charlie Ream gave OSU fans something about which to get excited.

for anything. I can't remember what I did with the money, but I probably went out to eat—something like Chinese food because it was cheap."

The Game

By Charlie Ream

Ohio State at Notre Dame—November 2, 1935

I don't remember much about the first three quarters, but we were ahead 13-0 going into the last quarter. On their second field-goal kick, one of my good friends, Fred Crowe, a 6-foot-6 tight end from Pomeroy, blocked their field goal attempt. They later called that the "golden arm." He joked that he wanted his arm framed when he died.

Our lead was threatened throughout the game. Notre Dame had a halfback from Chicago named Andy Pilney. He had several 40- to 50-yard runs. At one point near the end, he was carried off the field with a serious injury, which really riled up the Notre Dame fans. They scored on a couple of his runs and got the score to 13-12. A guy named Shakespeare replaced him. Next, they kicked off, and … our halfback fumbled on the first play. They recovered the ball; and, two plays later, they won the game on a pass from Shakespeare to a guy named Millner.

The Aftermath

While Ream may have been honored to be on the field that day, a loss is still a loss.

"It was devastating. The crowd was stunned at the last-minute touchdown. I think people just sat there. Everything went quiet. Later, I remember going into classes and professors saying something about the game. Everyone talked about it. I was pretty down in the dumps, but happy that I had a chance to play."

For Ream, just playing in that game was his college legacy.

"I [primarily] wanted to get an education, and then to play football at a bigger school. I had listened to all of Ohio State's games on the radio. I always thought I would like to play for that team, even though I was also hoping to get recruited by Notre Dame. But Notre Dame didn't recruit me, and neither did Ohio State. However, a doctor in my hometown, Dr. Underwood, thought I could play football at Ohio State. He knew someone who worked in the bursar's office [at Ohio State], and they helped me get to school and helped me find a job while I was there—this was long before scholarships. My first job was checking boots and hats in the men's gymnasium for 50 cents an hour. I stayed in the Tower Club, which was for kids who did not have much money. I think I paid about $12 [a month] for room and board, and I ate well there."

Ream went on to the U.S. Navy. As a member of the Navy's Iowa City Pre-Flight School team, he got on the field with the Buckeyes again—as an opponent. He eventually returned to Columbus, married, and went to work for Lazarus Department Stores. He lost his first wife and retired from Lazarus in 1975. He remarried in 1982.

Ream's sports career ended several years ago when his knees decided to retire from golf. Aside from the occasional swim in the Columbus Country Club pool, his only sports outlet is Buckeye football.

"Ohio State football and the university have been very good to me. I got a lot out of the university and appreciate everything that came from being a Buckeye."

27

KEN KUHN

BIRTH DATE: August 19, 1954
HOMETOWN: Louisville, Ohio
RESIDENCE: Pataskala, Ohio
POSITION: Linebacker
HEIGHT: 6-foot-2
WEIGHT: 230 pounds
YEARS: 1972 to 1975

A former high school All-American and Stark County (Ohio) MVP. ... A four-year letterman at OSU, where he was co-captain his senior season. ... Toyed with the idea of playing college basketball for Lefty Dreisell at Maryland, or football for Michigan until Woody Hayes issued an ultimatum: "He said he would fire my brother, Dick, who was a graduate assistant, if I didn't sign with Ohio State."

The Run-up

This is not an ordinary game of one's life. Ken Kuhn said it was to be the solution for unfinished business. This was Ohio State's fourth-consecutive trip to the Rose Bowl, and he said he firmly believes the Buckeyes should have won at least two of the previous games.

"This was Woody [Hayes] versus Dick Vermeil—*again*," Kuhn said. "We had beaten UCLA [41-20] in a Saturday night game in Los Angeles earlier in the season. We just wanted to go back out there and take care of business—finally."

Kuhn said the overture to the game actually began shortly after the regular season-ending, come-from-behind 21-14 victory against Michigan. The Buckeyes were outright Big Ten Conference champions and were a consensus No. 1 in the nation.

"We stayed focused, knowing what was at stake," Kuhn continued. "There wasn't a lot of 'rah-rah' hype about this trip on the team. We had a bunch of seniors who were going to be making their fourth trip out there, so it was more determination to get the job done than anything. Get out there, take care of business, and get back home with a national championship. We just had this confidence about ourselves. We had every intention of going out there to win the game and the national championship."

Before departing Columbus, the team had practices at the French Field House on the OSU campus, more a track-and-field facility than anything, and certainly a relic from another time. "The turf there was terrible," Kuhn said, "and with the ceiling you couldn't do much with your kicking game."

But California and all its glamour beckoned, as did the elusive national championship, and so the Buckeyes packed their bags, said their goodbyes, and headed for Port Columbus International Airport. The plane ride westward was uneventful, Kuhn remembers. There was no viewing of OSU or UCLA game films. "It was a long, four-hour flight, but it was pretty relaxed. Some of us slept, some played cards. Some read; you always took a book with you on trips—homework or at least something to read, regardless of whether you read it—because Woody would get on you if you didn't have it with you."

When they landed at LAX, Kuhn said it hit him for the fourth consecutive time: *I'm not going to be able to spend Christmas with my family again.*

"We had to leave our homes and families, wives and girlfriends—even though it was quite an honor to be there. There's just something about Christmas away. ... I don't know," he said, his voice trailing.

The surroundings and the various schedules were familiar to Kuhn and his senior classmates. Perhaps there was something to be said for routine. "Same hotel [Huntington Sheraton], same junior college [Azusa Pacific] for practice ... two full weeks of practice before the game, same trips to Disneyland and Johnny Carson's *Tonight Show* [taping]. I just wanted to play the game, win, play in the Senior Bowl, and come home by that point.

"But practices were very upbeat and positive," Kuhn said, adding, "and maybe a little intense. We [seniors] wanted to end our Ohio State careers by taking full advantage of bringing back the first national championship since 1968. We knew we had other opportunities, and they didn't work out."

Kuhn said he roomed with defensive tackle Nick Buonomici, "... and our room became a sort of 'gathering point.' We played some poker, watched some TV, and drank some Pepsis."

The Game
By Ken Kuhn

Ohio State vs. UCLA
The Rose Bowl—January 1, 1976

After our pregame meal, everyone was focused on what lay before us. When our bus arrived at the Rose Bowl, my parents were there to greet me. They were always there, and it always made me feel so good.

As we neared kickoff, I was more focused and more businesslike. After all, we were mature seniors playing our final game with the

Ken Kuhn rose to the top, battling through injuries and adversity.

opportunity to step it up to the next level. That was definitely in the back of my mind. This was the game of my life.

I took it all in. It was a beautiful, sunny day, but I wanted to get it over with, get done what we needed to do and get out of there. We had this confidence about it, because we had beaten them significantly out there earlier in the season, and I thought, overall, that we were the better team. Yet, even though we were undefeated and ranked No. 1—with Archie Griffin—this was no easy game. I don't remember the finer details since we lost 23-10, but there was a point where (safety) Craig Cassady intercepted (UCLA quarterback) John Sciarra, and I threw a hellacious block on whoever it was. We were on their side of the field with a chance to get back into the game. It should have been a rallying point.

On the next play, our quarterback, Cornelius Greene, dropped back to pass and let fly, but right into a UCLA defender's hands. The game, for all intents and purposes, was over in the first half. It sticks in my craw to this day. We should have won that game. When he set up to pass, I was standing on the sideline, saying, "No, Corny! No!" It's almost like he threw it right to the guy, but I believe to this day it was unintentional. I would never think Corny would do something like that intentionally.

So the game of my life ended with another loss in the Rose Bowl and another lost national championship. We could have had three. What an amazing letdown.

I have a brother, Richard Kuhn, a brother-in-law, Mark Stier and a cousin, Dustin Fox, each with an Ohio State national championship ring. Every time I see those rings, it hurts. Every season, I think about it.

This game has stuck with me since January 1, 1976, and it will stick with me the rest of my life.

The Aftermath

Ken Kuhn didn't get his hoped for—and many would say much-deserved—shot at one of the postseason college all-star games. "I flew back to Columbus with everyone else, while Archie, Corny, Brian Baschnagel, and others played in those games," he said. "It was supposed to be the trip home with a national championship trophy to give Woody Hayes, who was going to retire, which I believe he would have done had we won."

Injuries cut short his bid for a career in pro football, and so he began a career in sales, and today, he is a project manager for J and D Basement Systems in Columbus and central Ohio. He and his wife, Susan, have two sons, Nathan, 21, and Jake, 18.

How would he like to be remembered as a Buckeye football great?

Says Kuhn: "A tough, bull-headed—not unlike Woody—player who gave his all, who played through his pain and injuries, and who strove to be respected and liked by his peers."

28

KIRK LOWDERMILK

BIRTH DATE: April 10, 1963
HOMETOWN: Salem, Ohio
RESIDENCE: Kensington, Ohio
POSITION: Center
HEIGHT: 6-foot-3
WEIGHT: 262 pounds
YEARS: 1981 to 1984

Lowdermilk was one of the last in his class to be recruited by Ohio State—in fact; only two other schools recruited him. He wasn't recruited until he won his state wrestling championship match for Salem High School. He went on to play 12 years in the NFL with the Minnesota Vikings and Indianapolis Colts.

The Run-up

Rather than worry about taking on the top-ranked Sooners—and their sensational freshman tailback, Marcus Dupree—on their home turf in front of tens of thousands of rabid OSU fans, Earle Bruce's team got down to work.

"The coaches didn't say much during the week. Everyone understood how good they [the Sooners] were. We knew we would have to work hard at stopping them. We know how good their linebackers were, but we were ready," Lowdermilk remembered. "On the way into Oklahoma's stadium, the crowd was loud and obnoxious. They were ranked No. 1 in the country and were full of themselves; however, after the first few drives, the crowd completely quieted down and stayed that way for the rest of the game."

The Sooners and their loud fans weren't the only things with which Lowdermilk and his teammates had to contend.

"They put a thermometer on the Astroturf for the television audience, and when we went on the field it registered 105 degrees (it was believed to have reached 135 degrees later in the game)."

Lowdermilk, a recruiting afterthought by Bruce and his staff, was ready for his first big start, but he admits to being anxious before kickoff.

"I was a bit uptight going into the game. All week long, we'd heard the hype about Oklahoma, and Ohio State was considered to be the underdog. For Ohio State to be called an underdog going against anybody, it became a test of pride to be called an underdog. I think we responded really well to the test."

The Game

By Kirk Lowdermilk

Ohio State at No. 1 Oklahoma—September 17, 1983

By no means was the 24-14 victory a cakewalk.

John Frank wasn't supposed to play because of the Jewish holiday, Yom Kippur. The press made a big deal about John not playing. But he came out and had a heck of a game. I remember he had some long catches and then caught the first two touchdown passes.

I remember our line missed the block when we were in scoring position on the goal line. We got waylaid on the one- to two-yard line, and we were late off the ball and missed the block. Our running back got tackled for a loss down at the goal line. We couldn't score the touchdown and had to go for the field goal, which Richie Spangler got. It was a race between Earle and assistant coach Glen Mason to get to us to chew us out. Mason won.

Curt Curtis had a really good game. He had several sacks, some tackles for losses, and maybe recovered a fumble. I remember one of their players in the paper the next day saying, "Who in the hell is Curt Curtis?" I remember thinking, "He's just the guy who beat the crap out of you guys." It just sort of represented their whole attitude.

The Aftermath

"Everyone was excited, but really tired," Lowdermilk added. "Some guys cramped up really bad on the bus from the exhaustion and the heat. We had to get some IV bags, which sort of overshadowed some of the excitement about winning the game.

"I remember talking to one of the coaches after the game about how happy Earle was that he was able to beat Oklahoma. This was the first time that he was able to give them a good run for their money. He hadn't been able to beat them when he was at Iowa State, because he said didn't have the personnel that he had at Ohio State. It was such a big win for Earle, but he contained himself."

The next Monday, Lowdermilk found out what was expected of Buckeye football players.

"I remember coming off that great win and learned a lot about coaching philosophy that week. We beat the No. 1 team soundly, and

Kirk Lowdermilk prided himself on always being prepared to play.

then you go into the film room. ... I was totally shocked at how I was treated, how the whole offensive line was treated. We had all graded out pretty well, but Coach Mason brought us right back down to earth to get us ready for the next game, very quickly in fact. Our mistakes were pointed out just as strongly as the things we did well, maybe even stronger.

"I can remember that plain as day—the first time going through that whole thing and feeling so proud of your accomplishments, only to have the coaches bring you back to reality and to prepare you for the next week's game," continued Lowdermilk. "That's when it hit me that there's a big difference playing high school ball and playing Big Ten ball."

The pinnacle of Big Ten football came Lowdermilk's senior year, when Ohio State won the Big Ten and went to the Rose Bowl for the first time in five years. He went on to play 12 years in the NFL with the Minnesota Vikings and Indianapolis Colts. He now owns a tree farm with 400 acres called Viking Farms.

"We grow evergreen trees, dig them, and sell them to landscapers and nurseries. I bought the farm about the fourth or fifth year in the NFL. We were selling trees before I retired."

Lowdermilk has been happily married to his high school sweetheart, Kellee, since 1985. They have four children: Ashley, 20, a college sophomore and basketball player; Ally, 17, a softball pitcher; John, 13, a football fanatic; and Taylor, 11, who plays basketball and softball. When he's not tending to the tree farm or watching his kids compete, he likes to hunt.

Just being a part of Ohio State gridiron history is an honor for Lowdermilk.

"I guess I would have to say that I'd like to be remembered as a guy that was never as talented as the other players, by that I worked hard, persevered, and was ready. While other guys might have worked as hard as I did, no one worked harder than I did."

29

VIC KOEGEL

BIRTH DATE: November 2, 1952
HOMETOWN: Cincinnati, Ohio
RESIDENCE: Dallas, Texas
POSITION: Linebacker
HEIGHT: 6-foot-1
WEIGHT: 214 pounds
YEARS: 1971 to 1973

Koegel played high school ball for Gerry Faust, who went straight from Cincinnati Moeller High School to succeed Dan Devine as Notre Dame's head football coach. ... Koegel was All-Big Ten and a high school All-American. ... Koegel was a 12th-round draft pick in 1974 by the Atlanta Falcons before signing as a free agent with the Cincinnati Bengals.

The Run-up

Many good story lines surrounded the 1974 Rose Bowl—USC's Anthony Davis versus OSU's Archie Griffin; Ohio State being voted into the game by the Big Ten after tying with Michigan in the final conference game; USC's 42-17 drubbing of the Buckeyes in the 1973 game.

Yet, what Vic Koegel remembers the most is Woody Hayes.

"The team and Woody, we had a lot of pressure—high stakes to win, especially since the Big Ten had lost four times in the past four years," Koegel recalled. "Woody had lost two of those years. In fact, the last time we had won was with the 1968 national championship team. Southern Cal had beaten us the year before—had killed us the year before. They were the national champions of 1973. They had only lost one game out of the last 28 they had played. [The 1973 Rose Bowl] was when Woody had shoved the face of the cameraman [ABC's Mike Freeman]. Woody had left California with a subpoena. So there was a lot of pressure on poor Woody."

The team traveled out to Pasadena on December 20, and things just got worse.

"They took us to the *Tonight Show* with Johnny Carson," he said. "Jerry Lewis, the guest host, was the Hollywood type that Woody just despised, and he taught film at Southern Cal. We were all up in the stands, and they bring out Woody from the green room or wherever. He was very cordial. Jerry said, 'Coach Hayes, do you mind if I call you Woody?' and Coach said, 'Sure.' So Jerry said, 'You can call me Mr. Lewis.' From that point out, you could see Woody getting steamed. He was still very cordial because he was on Jerry Lewis' show … but you could tell he wasn't happy.

"Afterwards, we all get on the bus," Koegel continued. "We're sitting on the bus, and there's no Woody. We're waiting and waiting, and still no Woody. We're thinking he got a ride back. So we're on the east side and drive around the west side, and there's Woody standing in his suit with his briefcase, where he's been standing for an hour. He told the bus driver to pull around. He went nuts and threw his

Vic Koegel said the Rose Bowl was a pressure-packed affair for the Buckeyes, most especially Woody Hayes.

briefcase down, screaming, 'Get us out of here!' This was the pregame build up. I loved playing for Woody!"

The Game

By Vic Koegel

Ohio State vs. USC
The Rose Bowl—January 1, 1974,

Coach Hayes wasn't any happier on Game Day. They had beaten us 42-17 the year before; at halftime, the score had been 7-7, and they came out in the second half and just drilled us. This time, the score at halftime was 14-14, so we came out of the locker room all even.

Southern Cal began the second half of the 1974 game in an eerily familiar way. The Trojans opened the third quarter with an 83-yard touchdown drive to give USC a 21-17 lead.

Woody was going berserk. Unfortunately, (OSU linebacker) Arnie Jones was too close to Woody, and Woody punched him. Well, Arnie punched him back, and there was a little pushing going on. Woody was saying, "This is the same thing that happened last year! You're not going to let this happen again!" He went over to the offense and screamed at them and got everyone fired up. From that point on, we just dominated the whole game.

They didn't score another point. Our defensive coordinator, George Hill—probably the best defensive coordinator in the country—put together a defense that really shut down (USC quarterback Pat) Haden, and (USC wide receivers Lynn) Swann and (J.K.) McKay. Sometimes we'd rush three guys, sometimes four, and we'd drop four. They really couldn't get it together with our defensive strategy. We'd rush three, drop eight; do five short, three deep. There were times when I would spy everywhere Haden would go. We'd always have one guy there for the draw. We'd drop two defensive ends, too, so we'd have three guys and the middle linebacker would rush, plus the two defensive tackles. Pete Cusick had a number of sacks that day. He was an All-America defensive end, and he was the defensive player of the game. USC didn't know what to cover.

That was Pete Johnson's debut as an Ohio State starter, and he just ran over people. We had an 80-yard drive, and he scored a one-yard touchdown. Our next drive was 70 yards, and he scored another one-yard touchdown. Then there was 67-yard drive, and he had a four-yard touchdown. So you can see how we'd just rammed the ball down their throats.

There were big plays, too. Neil Colzie had a punt return of about 56 yards "… that really turned the game around." Archie Griffin added a 47-yard touchdown dash. Cornelius Greene, the sophomore quarterback, was named the game's MVP, aided in part by four big catches by lumbering tight end Fred Pagac to keep scoring drives alive.

The Aftermath

The victory was sweet, and the losers were gracious.

"After the game, we all get in the locker room. Lynn Swann walked in to congratulate us, which I thought was pretty classy on his part," Koegel said. "He came in, said a few words, shook some hands, and then went back into his locker room. When we got back to Columbus, the airport was packed with people. When we came off the plane, they had all these taxicabs driving us through. I just happened to get in the car with Archie. I was looking at all these people coming up to the car and wondering why—that's when I noticed Archie was in the car with me, and I realized who they were coming to see."

For Koegel and the other seniors, the win meant the end of their college lives. "I remember going up to Woody and thanking him for a great four years. Woody's speech always told the same story to the seniors. He'd say, 'I know you want to stay here, but you have to leave, you have to get on with your life.' I loved playing for Woody."

Koegel spent the fall of 1974 with the Cincinnati Bengals, and then moved on to life after football. He now owns and operates Koegel Training and Development in Dallas, which offers leadership training to companies like IBM. He's single and likes to play golf. Winning a

Rose Bowl wasn't the pinnacle of his football career; working towards that win was.

"I really wasn't a great one," Koegel said. "I was just surrounded by great players and coaches. I just played hard and was a team player."

30

GREG LASHUTKA AND IKE KELLEY

Editor's note: Teammates, co-captains and dear friends, Lashutka and Kelley requested their stories be combined, since the game of each man's life was the same game in their junior season at Ohio State.

BIRTH DATES:
Lashutka—March 28, 1944   Kelley—July 14, 1944
HOMETOWNS:
Lashutka—Cleveland, Ohio   Kelley—Bremen, Ohio
RESIDENCES:
Lashutka—Columbus, Ohio   Kelley—Columbus, Ohio
POSITIONS:
Lashutka—Tight end   Kelley—Linebacker
HEIGHTS:
Lashutka—6-foot-5   Kelley—5-foot-11
WEIGHTS:
Lashutka—240 pounds   Kelley—224 pounds
YEARS: 1963 to 1965

The Run-up

It's not quite enough to say everything was on the line when Ohio State traveled to Illinois for a game between unbeaten teams—with the winner absolutely having the inside track to the Rose Bowl. The year before, after the Buckeyes and Illini had tied at 20, Illinois got the Rose Bowl bid. That was a vicious punch in the gut for the Buckeyes—hard to handle, no chance of being forgotten, the stuff of grudges. Lashutka and Kelley were just two of several dozen in the Buckeyes' camp that circled this game on their schedules.

Illinois had 18 returning lettermen from that Rose Bowl squad, not to mention the overwhelming home-field advantage. Venerable Memorial Stadium was set to rock with Ohio State coming to town. To boot, it was the Illini's homecoming, and the hometown heroes had one nasty middle linebacker. No real introduction is needed, but for those scoring at home, he wore No. 51 on his jersey, and his name was Dick Butkus.

Said Kelley: "As Greg would point out, Mr. Butkus believed 'Ohio State is my meat.' Didn't turn out that way, though, did it?"

Kelley was an inside linebacker in OSU's 5-4 defensive alignment. Lashutka was a tight end, "... although I started out at split end, but then this kid named [Paul] Warfield—ever heard of him?—became the split end."

One wonders whether, considering the outcome of the previous season's matchup, Woody Hayes had his charges preparing for Illinois a little bit each week leading up to the full week of practice that normally would be dedicated to the game. "Other than Michigan, we didn't practice for any other team the week of the game," Lashutka said. "We just took them as they came."

Kelley does recall Hayes telling his squad of Butkus: "We'll hit him from the left, we'll hit him from the right; he'll never know which way we're coming from. We were the most physically and mentally prepared team I've ever come across in college or pro football. [Assistant coach] Esco Sarkinnen scouted all our opponents. For this game, and all the others, we were as fine-tuned as we could be. We knew everything Illinois was going to do. Kids were throwing up because they were so psychologically ready to take on the challenge. They had gone to the Rose Bowl; we didn't. We were ready. The nervous energy surfaced as soon as the kicker's toe hit the ball."

Added Lashutka: "Besides, Woody always put into context what a game was about—in this case, at the stadium where the legendary Red Grange played."

Kelley interrupted: "Playing on that field where someone of that magnitude did was daunting. I didn't think anyone could have beaten us that day."

And so the stage was set. The way Lashutka remembers, Game Day featured a "… perfect fall football setting. The sky was blue with crisp temperatures in the morning, warming to pleasant game-time temperatures for both the fans and the players. Minimal wind was in existence and much excitement in the air. The crowd was at full capacity at Memorial Stadium in Champaign, Illinois, all enthusiastically anticipating a great day and a great game between two Big Ten powerhouses, us and the Illini. The Illini fans were clearly in the vast majority, with the Orange and Blue showing throughout the crowd. The Illini fans attending the contest were most confident they would prevail in this highly touted game. A supportive, but small group of Ohio State football fans traveled to the game, but clearly were outnumbered in the stadium."

Lashutka said the football team traveled by air to Champaign the day before the game.

"We arrived in time for our usual workout the day before the game at the host stadium. Woody [Hayes] paused before we practiced to discuss the importance of the great Red Grange playing on the same football field we would play the next day and the importance of his contributions to the game of football. As always, Woody tried to put our games on the road into historical perspective. We enjoyed a pregame dinner on Friday at a local restaurant, which included a singing waiter who had in years past entertained Ohio State football teams. Since the game was in Illinois, the Land of Lincoln, it was appropriate for Woody to talk about Abraham Lincoln, one of his favorite historical persons. Woody discussed the many challenges Abraham Lincoln went through during his formative years which toughened his character, but certainly added to his dedication as a

Ike Kelley and Ohio State dominated Illinois—where and when it mattered most.

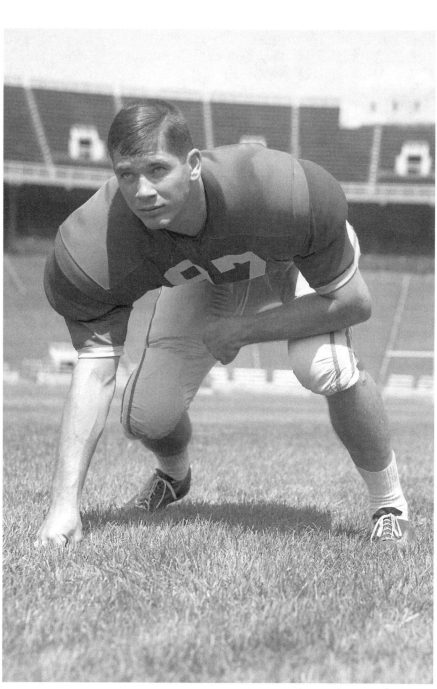

Greg Lashutka said he took away from this game yet another lesson: the challenges that would come in life after football.

leader exuding confidence, presence, determination, and a commitment of doing the right thing in his life. Woody analogized that Abraham Lincoln would have been a great tackle or tight end because of his height and size, as well as other attributes including his mental toughness."

The Game

By the combined voices of Greg Lashutka and Ike Kelley

Ohio State at Illinois—October 10, 1964

Many of the sports writers in attendance had given Illinois the nod as Big Ten Conference front-runners, because of their winning the Big Ten championship the year before and a great defense led by Butkus, as well as their offense led by Jim Grabowski. A timely *Sports Illustrated* cover story featured Dick Butkus. He was quoted as saying, "Ohio State is my meat. I like to play against them because they run right at you." That article and other media stories reflecting Butkus' enthusiasm to play against Ohio State—as well as our memories from the 1963 game—helped us prepare at a high level for this game.

Our offense focused on counter plays—faking one way and running the other—given the press statements of Dick Butkus, which would minimize his impact on our offensive strategy. Our defensive game plan was also well designed. Our preparation worked perfectly in the game. Also, as an incentive to our team, we prepared with great determination to avoid what occurred in 1963, to disallow that from happening again on the Illini gridiron. Our 26-0 victory set the stage for the next week when we played USC, which trounced us the year before.

There is always a particle of doubt. But the first three or four series of plays gave us an indication that it was going to be a great day no matter the outcome. The defense prevented anything from happening, and our offense scored the first three or four times we got the ball.

Football is a game of momentum, and that was clearly in our favor. We always played particularly well on the road, because it was us against the world.

You could not hear the crowd. We were having so much fun out there. It was the best. It would be great to play the game, way better than practice, and we had had a vigorous week of practice. Besides, it's more fun to hit somebody else.

"Communicate when necessary, but focus on your job," was the mantra in the defensive huddle. The offense, after the first series, had a confidence level that was very tight. It didn't matter which play was called; we were going to execute.

We had two tight ends on offense. Illinois ran a 6-1 defense, and Tom Kiefuss came in and wiped out Butkus. Tom Federle, our center, stood over him and said, "What's the matter, big boy, are we not running straight at you?" and our immediate thought was, "God, just don't piss that guy off."

The Aftermath

Kelley and Lashutka agree as to why this was the game of their lives.

"I think it's the game of my life because the team came together so solidly to perform the way we did," Kelley explained. "There were individual efforts that went above and beyond. From a team standpoint, we came together and put it together. I had double-digit tackles. Their quarterback was flushed from the pocket all day, and once I sent him sprawling into the bench, and I told him, 'You probably shouldn't be running the ball.'"

"Ike is understating again," Lashutka said. "The whole effort was something to behold. I don't [often] reflect on it, but very few have a chance to do what Ike and I did and do it well."

Lashutka said football is the consummate team sport. "That means 11 athletes attempting to execute each play with precision over a 60-minute sporting event in which the higher score ultimately beats the other team. Our preparation for the Illini game produced a victory and reinforced for most of us the lesson that hard work and sound preparation make a difference. Our thorough preparation of our offensive and defensive game plans, appropriate execution after much hard work before the game, and the importance of teamwork both on the field and in life paid great dividends. The satisfaction of our victory over Illinois was something all of us enjoyed on the way back to Columbus. That satisfaction continues to linger although somewhat faded with time yet today."

Kelley said he agrees, and added: "Your teammates become your best friends for life. Greg and I have stayed very close. We've tried [as a team] to have a reunion every five years, and the turnout has been great."

Lashutka said he took yet another lesson from this game—the challenge that would come in life after football. "Woody emphasized that we should take our lessons on the athletic fields and apply them to our life afterwards. I believe my greatest privilege was joining a great group of student athletes at Ohio State University, under a great coach, Woody Hayes, who gave me an opportunity to mature into manhood with many of the right lessons learned as a student athlete at The Ohio State University. Woody Hayes may not be properly understood by some, but to those of us who played for him he taught us lessons that endure today. Woody provided us important lessons in history, personal responsibility, the importance of teamwork, and the value of friendship that flowed from team members. He also taught us how, with hard work, we could overcome those with more talent but less desire."

Lashutka is a graduate of John Marshall High School in Cleveland, and he said his decision to go to OSU was rooted in "... the quality of the academics at Ohio State University and the opportunity to play for the great Woody Hayes over many other fine schools. I have not been disappointed by my choice."

He said his childhood included supportive teachers and family, and John Marshall had "... a wonderful college preparatory program and extracurricular activities, including sports, that were available and which I took advantage of during my formative years. My sports career included primarily football and basketball with a bit of track involvement, if they were really in need of people to participate."

These days, Lashutka, formerly the mayor of Columbus, is senior vice president for corporate relations at Nationwide. He has been married to Catherine Adams for nearly 25 years, and they have four children. Their oldest child, Nicholas, is married with two children. Lara is married with three children. Stephanie graduated from DePaul University in 2006, and Michael graduated from Columbus Academy in 2006. He enjoys a wide variety of interests and activities including reading, politics, and many outdoor activities including fishing, hunting, golf, cycling, and hiking. "I am also involved with a variety of non-for-profit activities at the local, state, and national level," he said.

Kelley was a top prospect coming out of the village of Bremen, Ohio, southeast of Columbus. "There were 45 people in my graduating class in 1962. I'm fortunate to have had the experience I did at Ohio State. Dick Elwood worked at Anchor Hocking nearby, and his brother, Frank, was recruiting me for Ohio State, Michigan, actually six Big Ten schools were recruiting me. It was not a good day for Michigan [as OSU won that game during his visit]. I made the decision right then and there. Besides, I wanted to be close to friends and family.

Kelley lived the country life growing up, having been reared on a 300-acre farm, where beef, dairy cattle, and hogs were the livestock. "I learned my work ethic there from my dad, with all the chores I had to do and the duties I was responsible for."

Kelley has been at Worthington Industries in the Columbus area for 33 years, beginning in sales for two years, and then going to the Corporate Human Resources Department for the next 31. That followed a seven-year run with the Philadelphia Eagles. He has been married to Barbara for 40 years, and they have two children, Brian and Kerrie, and six grandchildren, Max, Will, and Kate Orazen, and Collin, Anna, and Daniel Kelley. When he's not playing with the younger set in the family, Kelley said he loves to fish, hunt, golf, and involve himself with various charities in the local area by participating in fundraisers.

Each man said he would like to be remembered as a student-athlete who gave his all on the football field and in the classroom, as well as excelling at helping others to achieve.

31

VAUGHN BROADNAX

BIRTH DATE: June 22, 1962
HOMETOWN: Xenia, Ohio
RESIDENCE: Carmel, Indiana
POSITION: Fullback
HEIGHT: 6-foot-2
WEIGHT: 257 pounds
YEARS: 1980 to 1983

Broadnax was an all-league and Special Mention All-State player in high school. ... He participated in wrestling, track and field (high jump, long jump, shot put, discus, 100 meters and 200 meters. "I was the 'EverReady' guy," he said. ... "I didn't think football would earn me scholarship offers until after my junior year. I then had to decide whether I would wrestle in college, play football, or both. My favorite sport was wrestling, and I knew I would do well at the collegiate level. It was my success on the mat that brought out the football recruiters."

The Run-up

Not since the mid-1970s, when Ohio State bade farewell to All-America fullback Pete Johnson, had the Buckeyes enjoyed the presence of a human battering ram in the offensive backfield.

Enter Vaughn Broadnax. Buckeye faithful are glad he chose football.

It was warm on Game Day in Columbus, with temperatures up in the 80s on the field, fitting for a team from Texas being coached by the legendary Grant Teaff. For football, Broadnax said, "It was a good day. It was a sellout crowd, as was usual at the time. It was loud and boisterous. Everyone was getting ready for the new season."

Coming into this early season game was something of a pain to Broadnax, who was suffering through a nasty case of shin splints. "I was hobbled. … I wasn't doing the after-practice runs, so they would heal. I was wondering how long I would be able to play in the game."

His Buckeye teammates, though, were confident.

"As a team we thought we were going to have a good season," Broadnax said. "We had a good nucleus of players returning. We had lost our quarterback, Art Schlichter, and we were in search of a replacement. I think Mike Tomczak won the job outright. But there was still a question of whether he was going to be the quarterback to lead us the rest of the season."

He said the days leading up to this game, as was the case with all others, were fairly predictable.

"Typically, pregame was pretty structured the same all four years," Broadnax explained. "The traveling numbers, or the starters, were in lockdown from after practice on until after the game. We would have a light practice run-through Friday afternoon, then we'd bus to the [Ohio State] golf course for dinner. After dinner, we'd generally go to see a movie to get us to relax, or fired up, depending on the movie. After the movie we'd go to the hotel, and we would have some meetings and watch film. We'd have our customary snacks, something like soda and cookies. Then we would go to our rooms. In the morning, we would get up early to get taped in the hotel meeting

Vaughn Broadnax made the most of his opportunity versus Baylor.

rooms. Then there was the pregame walk around the hotel where we were staying. It was just a brisk walk, but we were usually in our suits. Coach [Earle] Bruce wanted us to look nice, so we looked nice walking around the neighborhood. After the walk, we'd have our pregame meal, which was typically a small steak and eggs, toast with butter, no jam or jelly, but we could have honey."

They were getting into a game-time frame of mind in this, his junior season.

"The summer leading up to my junior year I was in flux," Broadnax said. "Ever since I arrived at Ohio State I had wanted to play defense. I bugged the coaches repeatedly to let me play defense. They finally put me in at middle guard during the spring practice. And I thought I played pretty well, at least well enough for them to wonder whether I would remain at fullback or be on the defensive line. I always told them I could do both, but they weren't considering let me go both ways. There was a huge effort in July, when the coaches were seriously considering putting me in on the defensive line. But I know that [tailback] Tim Spencer was voicing his concerns, saying that he needed me as a blocker. I know some of the coaches also thought that I would be more valuable to the team on offense. So, I was kind of in flux.

"I enjoyed the summer, not having to worry about my weight, and I came into fall camp a little heavy. We had qualifying times for the half-mile run and the two-mile run. I easily made the times for the linemen, which I thought I was going to be, but I didn't make the time for the running backs. So I had to get up early every morning and run the qualifying times. I got the half-mile out of the way, but the two-mile was a struggle. For two weeks, I had to do that, in addition to the two-a-day [practices]. So I got into better shape, but it probably caused my shin splints."

Still, when it was time to play, Broadnax was definitely ready.

The Game

By Vaughn Broadnax

Baylor at Ohio State—September 11, 1982

With the question of my playing defense or offense, everyone was focusing on my blocking ability. I told them if they gave me a chance to run, I could do a pretty good job running the ball. The coaches always laughed when I told them that if they gave me the ball, they would see positive results.

Watching the films for Baylor, I knew they weren't going to hold our offensive line and our running game, despite their having an All-America linebacker. So all week, I'd say, "Let me run the ball, let me run the ball." I wanted to prove to my teammates and coaches that I could be an effective running back, aside from blocking.

Coach Bruce told me before the game, "We're going to run you today."

I told him I was ready. Some days you feel like nobody can stop you. This was one of those days for me. When I was near the goal line … I felt like nobody was going to stop me. Sometime in the first quarter, on my first carry near the goal line, it was a three- or four-yard run in. I got the ball and was immediately hit on the line of scrimmage by two Baylor defenders. Soon it became three and then four. And I just pulled them on through for the touchdown. That was just the way the game went for me that day.

The second touchdown I scored was very similar. It was probably in the second quarter. It was like they knew I was going to get the ball. I was greeted at the line of scrimmage by the defense, but I was still able to punch it in, carrying the defenders with me. My first two touchdowns gave the appearance that it was going to be a blowout. It was 14-0. But, we had a lot of turnovers, which made it a close game. Baylor was able to capitalize on our turnovers and score.

There were also a couple of runs that also stand out," he said. "During one, late in the second quarter, I think, I had about a 25-yard gain. That time I carried a defender for about 20 yards. I was dragging him along. He had a hold of my jersey and my shoulder pads. [Former tailback turned TV commentator] Jeff Logan later said something to the effect that there was a Brahma Bull Riding Contest in Ohio Stadium today. The guy was just holding on to me, and I was dragging him down the field until his teammates caught up to me. Unfortunately, someone on our side fumbled the ball a couple of plays later, so it was all for naught.

Another play I remember was when we were at the goal line, and I was given the same play. Baylor jumped offsides, and I didn't get to run for the third touchdown. We ran the quarterback sneak instead, since we had gotten half the distance to the goal (as a result of the penalty). We scored on that one, as well.

I was blocking for Tim Spencer as well. (Spencer had 147 yards rushing, while Broadnax had 101.) We had a good offensive rushing game. We knew we were going to have a good running game because Baylor was kind of smallish. Not only did we have a big backfield, but we had a big offensive line. We knew we could do some damage against them. On their offense, they had a star player, a flanker, Gerald McNeil, whose nickname was "The Flea." He had to be 5-foot-8, 147 [pounds]. He was a great player."

During this game, we had unveiled a split-back formation, which I loved because Tim was able to block for *me* at times. It gave us opportunities to go to either side of the line depending on the defense. I could block, be a lead blocker and Tim could be a lead blocker. We had counter plays out of that formation, which confused the defense, because, generally, they were following my steps as lead blocker, and they would follow me. If we had called counter, they were in that motion and we would cut back the other way, and we would have good gains. So, during this game, we unveiled a new wrinkle in our offense, which we used a lot afterwards, because it worked well."

This game solidified my being able to run the ball effectively and open the eyes of many coaches on my team and other teams that I could be a threat running the ball. That was something I always wanted to prove at Ohio State, given the long tradition of fullbacks. I knew my role as a blocker, but sometimes the blocker wants to get "a little cheese."

The Aftermath

In the end, Ohio State prevailed and escaped Baylor's upset big, 21-14.

Any jubilation over the victory against the Southwest Conference opponent was tempered by the fact that the Buckeyes weren't taking care of the ball the way they should, the way they prepared to do it, the way they were taught to do it.

"The end of the game was kind of anticlimactic, because we had so many turnovers and so many mistakes," Broadnax said. "The game shouldn't have been that close. So it was more of a relief that we pulled it off."

Off the field, away from the raucous crowd, Broadnax had time to think about what had transpired. "For me, sometimes during a game you can experience a good play and you know it was a good play, but you can't visualize it, you can't see it," he said. "It's not until you see the actual replays that you appreciate the magnitude of some of the plays. And that's what happened to me after this game. We were able to watch the replay on WOSU-TV [and later on the films on Sunday], and I was able to see some of the plays and hear the comments of Jeff Logan. That's when I saw how effective some of my running was."

Inasmuch as this was a breakout game for Broadnax, it was something else that left him unbelievably satisfied.

"No, it was graduating in four years," he said of his greatest accomplishment at Ohio State. "I enjoyed football immensely, but it was always the vehicle for other avenues for me." Broadnax didn't necessarily see Ohio State as an option coming out of Xenia.

"Before my junior year in high school, my goal was to go to the Naval Academy," he said. "But I took a visit [to Annapolis, Maryland] in my senior year, and I realized that I didn't want to go there. The facilities were in bad shape. The locker room, the equipment was terrible. Plus, I would have had to deal with the regimentation of being a *plebe*, and that didn't look so great up close. My mother supported me through all of my dreams of going to the Naval Academy. When I rejected the appointment, she was kind of ticked off and didn't talk to me for two weeks after I signed with Ohio State. Notre Dame and Ohio State were my final two choices. My mother came around after my graduation at Ohio State—that was all she wanted. Everyone in my hometown was pushing me to go to Ohio State. I really liked Ohio State's wrestling coach [Chris Ford] and was considering wrestling. Plus, Ohio State had a really good engineering program that I was interested in. So those were factors that swayed me in favor of Ohio State."

With football in his wake, Broadnax today is a veterinary sales manager with Iams, the pet food company. He handles getting the company's prescription line of diets to the veterinary community.

"My wife is Josephine. My daughter is three, and [was] aptly named Carmen in celebration of our national championship in 2002 [when Ohio State withstood Miami's last charge for a heart-stopping, double-overtime, 31-24 victory in the Fiesta Bowl]."

Broadnax busies himself in his spare time by singing in Circle City Sound, a barbershop harmony chorus, shooting pool, playing cards, playing golf, fishing, cycling, and cooking. And, he added, "I also officiate at track and field [events]." He is a certified official with a goal of officiating in the Olympics. He also is vice-president of the Indianapolis chapter of NFLPA retirees and active with the NFL Alumni, and he is active in his fraternity, Phi Beta Sigma. Further, he is on the board of directors for the Starfish Initiative, an organization that identifies highly motivated and talented students that would benefit from private-school placement.

As to how he would like to be remembered as an Ohio State football great, Broadnax said this: "Most people would remember me for the 1981 Michigan game, where I had the block that helped us win the game."

With time winding down, Broadnax flattened a Michigan defender, allowing Ohio State quarterback Art Schlichter to get loose for the winning touchdown. Ohio State's 14-9 conquest denied Wolverines the Rose Bowl bid.

Asked by *Varsity O* to characterize that play, Broadnax said, "Many times as a player you try to just do your job until the whistle. But, I also heard the OSU crowd in the end zone starting to roar, and I knew something was happening. The importance of my block was not realized until after returning to the sidelines, and Art thanked me for giving him so much time. There weren't any replay screens at that time, so I really didn't think it was that special other than the fact the touchdown gave us the lead.

"If that's the mark that I left, then I'm happy that I left a positive mark for my years at Ohio State."

Broadnax still is connected to Ohio State football. As recently as 2004, he was asked to be an honorary captain at the Michigan game. "It was a great honor. Being able to be involved with the team, even just a little bit, for the Michigan game was overwhelming," Broadnax told *Varsity O*. "Sharing a thought with the team during the pregame meal was just an unbelievable experience. Standing at midfield for the toss was outstanding, but when the team kicked Michigan's tail, I couldn't have written a better script for a Saturday in November."

32

BRIAN BASCHNAGEL

BIRTH DATE: January 8, 1954
HOMETOWN: Pittsburgh, Pennsylvania
RESIDENCE: Chicago, Illinois
POSITION: Wingback
HEIGHT: 6 feet
WEIGHT: 195 pounds
YEARS: 1972 to 1975

Academic All-America and Academic All-Big Ten choice as well as a National Football Foundation Hall of Fame Scholarship winner in 1975. ... Graduated from OSU with a business degree in administration and finance. ... In high school, he loved basketball, but his football and basketball coaches had a conflict about his availability, so Baschnagel opted for volleyball. ... Was third-round pick of Chicago Bears in 1976, where he played 10 seasons as a wide receiver.

The Run-up

Brian Baschnagel always had visions of becoming a big-time running back in a major college football program—just not at Ohio State.

"The one team I really could identify with was Notre Dame. I was a big 'Domer.' I was recruited by Notre Dame, Penn State, Michigan, Ohio State, and some other Big Ten schools, but I didn't want to go to Ohio State. I was an O.J. Simpson fan and had watched Ohio State beat USC in the [January 1, 1969] Rose Bowl. I just didn't want to [visit] there, although there was no reason not to go. ... Woody, as he always was, was quite involved in recruiting. He did a lot of personal visits [to prospects' homes and schools]. He called me and said, 'Brian, I'd like to take you out to dinner.' This was prior to my visit in 1972. He came out to Pittsburgh, and I said to him, 'Coach, I have volleyball practice.' He said, 'No problem. I'll come to the school. I'll wait for you.'

"Whenever I did something good at practice, I looked over to where Coach Hayes was sitting. He sat on a bench the whole time and read a book, *Animal Farm*. I don't think he ever looked at me. After practice was over, I took a quick shower, and we went out to dinner. ... We never discussed football. He sold me on the business school, the law school."

Baschnagel visited 10 schools. He said in the back of his mind, he was bound for Notre Dame.

"Before Woody visited, Earle Bruce had been recruiting me. He called me when he left OSU to become the head coach at the University of Tampa. He told me Ohio State would be a great place for me. I thought that was classy. Then I developed a relationship with George Chaump, who was too nice of a guy, and I found I couldn't tell him 'No.'"

Knowing full well that he had to earn a spot on the team, that there were no guarantees, Baschnagel committed to Ohio State.

Archie Griffin changed Brian Baschnagel's (above) outlook on his college football career.

"I had done well running the ball at North Allegheny High School in Pittsburgh, and one of the reasons I went to OSU was because they ran the ball," Baschnagel said. "I mean, what better place to exploit my abilities? When I got to Columbus for summer camp, I was with eight other tailbacks. We ran the I-formation, with a tailback and a fullback."

As preseason camp ensued, each tried his best to impress Woody Hayes. "We all tried to work our way up, and as freshmen, we were *all* at the bottom of the depth chart."

In the first game of his freshman season, OSU stomped Iowa in Ohio Stadium. It was a remarkable day for the offense, but unremarkable for one of the freshmen. His name: Archie Griffin. He fumbled his first carry in the waning moments of the game as the scrubs were getting some playing time.

The Game

By Brian Baschnagel

North Carolina at Ohio State—September 30, 1972

When the North Carolina game started, our offense was doing nothing—and worse, we were losing. I'm not sure what the circumstances were there. Elmer Lippert either got hurt or the decision was just made to put Archie in there. He helped us to come from behind to win. I mean, he had 239 yards rushing, which was a single-game record at Ohio State.

So Archie goes ahead and helps us win. Not only did he do it in less than three quarters, but he became an overnight hero. I was happy that we came behind to win the game, but I had mixed emotions about where I fit in. Remember, I had high hopes coming to Ohio State. It's funny how you think as a freshman, but you realize at some point you have to earn the right to play; you have to beat out the other players. When they're upperclassmen, you live with it. When they're in the same class as you, you wonder, "What were the odds of playing tailback at Ohio State?"

I was very envious, jealous of Archie. I had negative thoughts. "Maybe he'll get hurt," I truly thought to myself. "Maybe he'll fumble or lose consistency."

I was immature and didn't understand. I "felt" like a team player, but I had these incredibly selfish individual things going through my head like, "Should I go to another school?"

This was after two games of my college career!

So Archie Griffin, deservedly, gets all kinds of attention, pats on the back. He's an overnight hero. It became salt in the wound to me. It really bothered me. I was selfish. My gut was just wrenching. I thought, "This is the end of my career here; no way I'm going to have any fun. How am I going to contribute?"

Obviously, I was very narrow-minded.

When we got into practice on that Monday, Archie Griffin didn't dress. My immature mind kicked in, and I thought, "He's milking this." They said he had bumps and bruises. I didn't buy that. That is the mentality I had.

He was reaping benefits, and he should have.

Then I got a huge wakeup call, and it didn't come from the Old Man, or even from one of the assistant coaches. After practice, we went into the weight room. I was the last one out of the facility, because, at that time, Ohio State was on the four-quarters system, and we hadn't started school, so there was no pressure, no homework. So I just hung around to get in extra work. I figured I needed to be in great shape, because I was wondering about transferring. In my mind, it had come to that. Archie Griffin might've been hurt, but I knew he was going to get better.

That day, I was last into the shower. Finally, Archie Griffin came in ... fully clothed, and he said to me, "I've been meaning to talk to you since Saturday. You're from Pittsburgh; had it been the other way around, you would have gone in and did what I did."

That overwhelmed me. He took the time to prove his sensitivity and awareness—and I promise you he wasn't wrapped up in his success. When I think about what he told me, to this day I do believe he believed that. You know, I didn't know him that well up to that point, but what he said to me completely changed my attitude about everything. All of a sudden, I stopped being selfish. I didn't care if I had to play behind Archie Griffin; it wouldn't be all bad. I knew we would be successful. He helped me take a completely different attitude.

Rick Galbos, a few games later, got hurt; and I became the starting wingback that season. That game and Archie's success changed my whole approach to playing at OSU and ultimately changed my marketability to the NFL.

The Aftermath

"There would have been no way for me to survive in the NFL as a running back," Baschnagel said. "At Ohio State, I had a durable career, and the experience helped me to develop my blocking skills— I still ran the ball some; they threw me some bones. We didn't throw the ball a whole lot, but we did, nonetheless, and I was able to develop receiving skills, get good at route running and gain development. It was a broader-based level of skills. I became a much more versatile football player. Maybe I wouldn't have had the opportunity, if not for Archie's game. Who knows? All I know is that it pushed me into the wingback spot very quickly, and it taught me to be a better football player. It enabled me to be an all-around football player. I learned to play more than just another role, because I held for extra points and field goals, and I returned punts and kickoffs. It developed me for the NFL. The Chicago Bears had me on special teams and at wide receiver. They tried me out at cornerback, and if they hadn't viewed me as an 'athlete,' they wouldn't have done that.

"I don't know if this game was my greatest accomplishment, but it was my greatest game for all the right reasons," Baschnagel admitted. "I'm not proud of the fact that I was very individualistic. After what Archie said to me, I had no more selfish thoughts. I was relieved to go to the wingback spot and then start every game.

"Archie taught me a major lesson, and I changed overnight."

Today, Baschnagel is the manager of marketing services for North American Corporation, a suburban Chicago distributor of a variety of disposable items; nearing 20 years with the company, he also oversees major accounts.

He and his wife, Mindy, have three children: daughters Mallory and Allie, and a son, Luke.

When he's not involved with his children's activities, he said he loves to exercise. "My knees are arthritic, but I ride the stationary bike. I 'entertain' myself 45 minutes a day with conditioning. I also play golf—although I'm not very good—about a dozen times a year."

Baschnagel wants to be remembered as "... ultimately, the team player that was concerned about the good of the team and not necessarily what was good for me, as a good student-athlete. I think I accomplished those things, and I was serious about academics."

33

MATT KELLER

BIRTH DATE: December 12, 1976
HOMETOWN: Cincinnati, Ohio
RESIDENCE: Cincinnati, Ohio
POSITION: Fullback
HEIGHT: 6 feet
WEIGHT: 240 pounds
YEARS: 1996 to 1999

Keller received a scholarship despite his mother wearing Cincinnati Moeller High School's team colors of blue and gold to his recruiting visit during the OSU-Michigan game. ... He is an inductee of Cincinnati Moeller's Athletic Hall of Fame for football and lacrosse. ... He served as Ohio State's co-captain with Ahmed Plummer his senior season.

The Run-up

Matt Keller thought everything looked good the morning of Ohio State's home game versus Illinois. The weather was perfect—chilly, but sunny. The Buckeye faithful were loud and lined along the streets of Columbus between the team's hotel and Ohio Stadium. He couldn't wait for kickoff.

"For any athlete, pregame was the worst thing ever," he said. "You're ready to go; you've been preparing all week; and then you have to wait. You get to the stadium two and a half hours early. I told myself, especially with this being my last home game, to soak it all in. It was so agonizing to wait because I was in the locker room, and I just wanted to go play. That day, however, everything seemed to go so fast. Before I knew it, I was on the field with the coin toss."

Keller got his moment in the chilly sun.

"One of the most special memories I have is when they recognized the seniors for the final game in the Horseshoe. It's such an honor," recalled Keller. "I remember when they called my name. I was the last guy to get introduced. I got all choked up when they announced my teammates' names, and then it was my turn. I told myself that I had to hold it together in front of 100,000 people. It was unbelievable to get that kind of recognition from 100,000 fans. I remember getting teary-eyed and putting my helmet on. I saw my parents on the field, and it was even harder to hold it in. I took off my helmet and turned around 360 degrees to make sure that I took it all in.

"Everything about that game solidifies the tradition, the town and the fan base in my mind. That's what makes Ohio State football so great. When they gave us a standing ovation, it was as if they were thanking us for all the hard work that we had put in. It was the biggest thank you. I wanted to thank the fans for supporting us all those years. You put all this hard work in, working your tail off with all these guys, and at the end, you know it was appreciated by these fans.

"After the introductions, you get to go to midfield to meet your parents. To be able to share that moment with them was wonderful. My folks were a very big influence in my life. Whether I was missing six games with a bad ankle or being third-string, they were always proud of me. That meant so much to me to be able to share that moment—probably one of the greatest of my life at this point—with my parents. They put a lot of work into raising me right and doing everything they could to help me before and during my years at Ohio State.

"My family, including my grandparents, aunts, uncles, cousins supported me throughout my college career," Keller said fondly. "After my redshirt year, when my parents went to every home game, they traveled to every game thereafter, home and away, as did many of my other family members. At the 1996 Indiana game, I had about 25 family members come watch me play."

The Game

By Matt Keller

Illinois at Ohio State—November 13, 1999

Reaching the end of that long, gratifying gridiron journey caught up with me on the field against the Fighting Illini.

Unfortunately, this game was not my personal best. There are so many things that happen on a football field. When you break the huddle, you get all the pre-snap reads as far as what defense they're in, what guy will blitz, what guy will I pick up, etc.

I was still focused on doing my job, but I couldn't help thinking this was the last time I was going to be out there for a coin toss as a captain. Next, I started thinking this was the last opening drive of my last game at the Horseshoe. Then I was reflecting that this was the last first series after half time—and on it went. You're looking at all your teammates thinking this was the last time you were going to see these guys. There was so much off-the-field work that you do with these guys—winter conditioning, where you're on the field at six in the morning running sprints, doing all kinds of crazy stuff. These were the things that were racing through my mind.

Matt Keller said he found his mind wandering during his last home game.

The game wasn't one to write home about. They jumped out to a 29-7 lead, and we were never in the game, losing 46-20; but it wasn't all bad.

Probably the most special thing that happened to me was that I caught a touchdown. The play was a fake run, where I act like I'm going to go run and hit the linebacker just like a regular running play. Quarterback Steve Bellisari faked the handoff to the tailback. I went to go block the linebacker. I acted like I was going to block him, then I slipped down the field, and I was so wide open it was unbelievable.

I started to get to the goal line, so I began to back peddle to give Steve a bigger and better target. I couldn't see Steve because of all those big linemen. All I could see was the ball coming. It was like slow motion. I can just remember watching the ball come into my hands.

I can remember landing in the end zone and the ball bouncing away from my chest. I put a death grip on that football to get it back down. It was almost like redemption to allow me to catch that ball that day.

I remember my teammates looking at me with a genuine feeling of happiness for me. To have them come congratulate me like they did, it was an awesome, awesome feeling.

The Aftermath

The home loss was tough. The 24-17 loss the next week at Michigan was tougher, as it knocked the 6-6 Buckeyes out of the postseason for the first time in more than a decade. But Keller's last appearance in Horseshoe will always be his favorite.

"Beating Notre Dame at Notre Dame was unbelievable, winning the 1997 Rose Bowl and beating Michigan were both wonderful," he said. "But nothing was as special as this last home game."

Keller is proudest of being named a co-captain. He credits that honor to the example he set for teammates.

"I think I want to be remembered as a blue-collar player," he said. "As someone who would do anything to get the job done. Everyone worked hard. I put my time in during the off-season; I watched the tapes; I did everything expected of me and then some more."

Keller is single and back home in Cincinnati now, working as a service sales rep for Cintas.

34

CRIS CARTER

BIRTH DATE: November 25, 1965
HOMETOWN: Middletown, Ohio
RESIDENCE: Boca Raton, Florida
POSITION: Split end
HEIGHT: 6-foot-3
WEIGHT: 194 pounds
YEARS: 1984 to 1986

In the 1985 Rose Bowl game, Carter nabbed nine catches for 172 yards, which was a then-Rose Bowl record. One of those receptions was for 18 yards and a touchdown in the fourth quarter. He was drafted by the Philadelphia Eagles in 1987, where he played for three years. When he was released from the Eagles in 1989, ESPN commentator Chris Berman remarked on the imprudence of Coach Buddy Ryan's decision and said, "All [Carter] does is catch touchdowns." The Minnesota Vikings picked him up, and Carter went on to play in eight consecutive Pro Bowls, became All-Pro four times, and held most of the Vikings career receiving records when he left in 2001. In 1999, he became the second player in NFL history to catch 1,000 passes (Jerry Rice was the first) and was named the NFL's Man of the Year. He also was part of the NFL's 1990s All-Decade Team.

The Run-up

What more could a Midwest resident want at the end of the year? With ice, snow, and a honking wind blowing out of the north, just getting around Columbus was, well … misery. Take one Ohio State football team out of those climatic elements, and you have a pretty happy bunch on your hands. Put those folks in sunny Southern California, and you've just one-upped yourself. And so it was with Cris Carter and the Buckeyes, who ventured forth to Pasadena for the granddaddy of them all—the Rose Bowl.

"It was a beautiful day. For us coming from the Midwest with the snow, it was the prettiest day on the prettiest stage that I had ever seen. The crowd made me feel like I was in Ohio Stadium. The shape, the structure was a lot like Ohio Stadium, but with just one level, not like the split-level. We always had a great following, but [Southern Cal] did, too.

"I remember how beautiful the grass was during pregame," Carter continued. "We didn't have an opportunity to practice on the field before the game, so that was our first shot at seeing it. Teams we had played previously that had grass had more of the Midwestern grass, the Kentucky blue grass, which is very thick and comes up in chunks. This was Bermuda grass or rye grass, which grows in more tropical places like Florida or California and feels smoother. Plus, the field was cut very thin. It was a very fast field."

Take one fleet-footed wide receiver and put him in those conditions, and, if you're the opponent, you're asking for trouble. It's like playing with matches near the gas can.

"I had a little chip on my shoulder because I really wanted to go to USC [out of high school]," explained Carter. "The coach that was recruiting me, Norv Turner [who went on to fame and infamy as an NFL coach], got snowed in at Kansas City and decided not to wait another day to come visit me. He decided to go back to California."

Whoops!

"So when he said he was going back to Los Angeles, I cancelled my visit to USC and decided not to go to school there," Carter said. "We

Cris Carter gained the confidence to dominate from his game of his life.

talked about this after the game. He said he deeply regretted not being able to make the visit, because [head coach] John Robinson told him the decision was up to him—he could come back to L.A. or wait a day and visit me the next day. He chose to go back home, and I chose to go to Ohio State. He ended up coaching me my last year in the NFL."

Hollywood did offer the young receiver a chance to mingle with stars, though.

"The opportunity to meet [then-NBC Sports commentator] Ahmad Rashad was unbelievable," Carter said. "It was my first time meeting him. I had a great deal of respect for him as a wide receiver. Talking to him before the game got me really pumped up. There was a lot of nervous energy, and I remember being very nervous. ... I was a freshman playing in the Rose Bowl."

Carter embodied the ultimate in preparedness, even as a fresh-faced first-timer.

"I remember staying up with my roommate the night before doing the visualization exercises that Coach [Earle] Bruce was always teaching us. I kept visualizing myself having an amazing game. USC had a great defense, a number of guys who went on to have great careers—guys like Tim McDonald, Jack Del Rio, and Duane Bickett. I knew we wouldn't be able to run the ball.

"So I knew, in order for us to win, we were going to have to throw the ball," Carter said. "The thing about Ohio State—and it took me a long time to understand this—was that no matter what kind of defense the other team had, we would always try to run the ball first. But I knew we weren't going to be able to run against USC's defense, so I took the time to prepare myself to make my contribution through the passing game."

The Game

By Cris Carter

Ohio State vs. Southern California
The Rose Bowl—January 1, 1985

Most people are surprised that I would choose this as the best game of my life because we lost, 20-17. However, it was more than just a game to me. For one thing, it was my only opportunity to play in the Rose Bowl, although at the time I thought that there would be many. When you get there as a freshman, and you think about the team that you know is coming back the next year, you think that you'll definitely be back one more year. But that didn't happen.

Secondly, this game had a tremendous impact on my total psyche as an athlete, which contributed to making it the game of my life. This game gave me the confidence that on the biggest stage I could call on my abilities and be able to answer them. And being at a young age, you think you have talent, and you can do certain things at practice, but mentally, until you get it on the inside of you, you're not there. I think this was the first time that I knew that I could be a great player.

This game was a springboard for me for my goals and what I wanted to accomplish at Ohio State more than any other game. I was also able to show people who were important to me, people like my brother (Butch, a former Indiana University and NBA player), that I had made the right decision to play for Ohio State.

During our first drive, (OSU tailback and Heisman Trophy contender) Keith Byars broke a big run, but Tim McDonald, an All-America safety, ran Keith down. We had never seen that. There's always a perception, especially in those days, that when you go to the West Coast, when you go to the Rose Bowl, that the Pac-10 has far more speed, far better athletes than the Big Ten. The Big Ten has more physical, "run the ball" strong guys, but the Pac-10 has better athletes. Seeing Keith run down from the back was something we had never seen before. He was the best athlete we had on our team, and it really shocked us.

They stopped us inside the 5-yard line, and then we missed the field goal. So starting off the game, we started off like we normally do. We were going to run the ball, Keith was going to make some plays. … But for them to stop us from getting any points at all, that changed the whole tone of the game—and that was the first drive of the game.

Early in the game in the first quarter, I got hit, and it was the first time I got hit so hard that I got dazed, and the trainer had to come out on the field and help me off. It was the legendary trainer from Ohio State, Billy Hill, who came over and had a few profane words for me once he figured out I was okay. I had just gotten my head dinged a little bit, and I was a little dizzy. Once he knew I was okay, he gave me a few choice words as far as what he thought of me. He thought I was trying to get out of the game, the big game—that I was intimidated in an easy fashion. I only stayed out a couple of plays.

I took another shot before halftime and got up from that. The potential of getting hurt was in the back of my mind. But, during some of the most crucial parts of the game, I made some critical plays. One was a third-and-long situation, catching the ball and converting the third down. We were trying to mount a comeback, and I scored a 17- or 18-yard touchdown on a low throw in between a couple of guys. I was able to scoop it up before it hit the ground in the end zone.

I remember thinking when Tomczak threw it, that the ball wasn't going to get to me or that it was going to be intercepted. That catch gave me a lot of confidence.

From a coaching-staff standpoint, and even from a team standpoint, they don't expect freshmen to make big plays in a big game—especially in the receiver position, where, because of the rules of football, we (receivers) were a necessary item. But Mike (Lanese) and I knew we could dominate. We knew we could make plays. Every time they called on us, we made those big plays. It was always puzzling to us why we had to get into critical situations and then be forced from an ideal standpoint to throw the ball.

At that time, my brother was playing in the NBA, and this was one of the few games he could watch. He was always my role model, and he was against my playing for Ohio State. He said they would never throw me the ball, that my talents would be better utilized playing basketball or going to a school that threw the ball. It was nice for me to be in the position to say, "Look, Ohio State is throwing the ball, and they are throwing it to me." So this game was also a confirmation for me that, "Yes, I am at Ohio State, and I did make the right decision. This was our potential, not only individually, but as a team."

It was probably the most physical game that I had ever been in. I remember how long halftime was with all of the festivities, which was good for me because it gave me time to recover. I felt like I had played in a whole game by halftime.

The first half of the game was very, very sunny. We hadn't played in a game with any sunshine for three months or more. I couldn't wait to get to halftime so I could refresh and get some nutrients in my body. I was utilized twice as much in this game as I had been all season.

The Aftermath

By and by, the sun started to settle into the Pacific horizon, and the game was completed under the lights. Though a Buckeye loss, the game promised unbelievable efforts by Carter, who walked dejectedly, hardware in hand, to the Ohio State locker room. As great as his individual game was, the team was all that mattered to him.

"I was disappointed," Carter said. "We replayed the game in our minds and saw where we made so many errors, but also had so many opportunities to win the game. [However], I was a freshman, and I knew that there would be many opportunities for me. I was cognizant of the difficulties facing the seniors who would be wearing the Buckeye uniform for the last time."

A somewhat silver lining—in wake of the outcome—was bestowed upon Carter.

"Even though we lost the game, I won the offensive MVP, which was unique. ... I had to stay on the field after the game to receive the trophy. Ahmad Rashad talked about that, how I was a freshman and we lost, but I still won the offensive MVP."

As amazing as this game was personally for Carter, the pinnacle of his playing days at Ohio State was represented by the first-team All-America honor he received two seasons later as a junior. "That was one of my goals. I remember when I visited Ohio State, and I saw the Buckeye trees [in a grove behind the south end of Ohio Stadium]. They told me that the only way you get a Buckeye tree was to be first-team All-America. At that time we had around 100 All-Americans [in the university's storied football history], and that was impressive, given the large number of great football players Ohio State had had. I made it my goal to become first-team All-America during my recruiting visit. And then I achieved it my junior year."

The odyssey to Columbus—one that didn't go through Pasadena—began when Carter was a senior at Middletown High School.

"I was having a long, bad day," he recalls. "Recruiters were everywhere we went. On that day, I was sitting at home having dinner with my mom. I told her I was tired of people asking me where I was going to go to school. She tried to explain to me that it was part of the process and that I should look at it in a different way. So I said to her that people don't care about her opinion; they never asked her where she thought I should go. She said, 'I've always dreamt of one of my kids playing for Ohio State.' I was the youngest of four boys, and the other three had gone off to play basketball, none had gone to Ohio State. So right then, in November, I decided, 'That's what I'm going to do; I'm going to listen to my mom and go to Ohio State.'

"I looked everywhere for advice—from my coaches, my brothers, my friends, people at universities. But what it all boiled down to was that I listened to my mom."

Even today, Carter didn't see that motherly advice, albeit in wish form, coming.

"... If you had told me that along the way, I wouldn't have believed you. I would have said, 'I'm going wherever I want to go,'" he said. "But it shows you that kids are listening to you even when you don't think they are.

"My mom wanted me to go to Ohio State because her dad had grown up being an Ohio State fan and being a football fan. But my family was a basketball family. Plus, she loved [former coach] Woody Hayes. She thought that what he did for young people was tremendous. She also liked Ohio State's staff. She liked Coach [Earle] Bruce, and she really liked Coach [Jim] Tressel; who was the one who recruited me. She liked how accountable they were, and what they promised her [about] off the field things is what really sold her."

Carter's prodigious high school career was the envy of many.

"[My] senior year, I [became] the first player ever voted first-team All-State (for) offense and defense, I was also a *Parade* [magazine] All-American and *USA Today* All-American."

For the record, the man who arguably is Middletown's most accomplished athlete ever also was named to the first team in All-State basketball.

As was the case when he was an athlete, Carter today is all over the place.

"In my spare time, I own a security company with my brother, John, called Carter Brothers. We specialize in commercial electronic security and operate out of Atlanta. I am also a host of *Inside the NFL* for HBO Sports [a distinction he shares with Dan Marino, Cris Collinsworth, and Bob Costas], and do my own radio show on Sirius Satellite Radio, and I write for YahooSports.com for their Internet content as the NFL expert. My most rewarding job, though, is as a high school football coach, the offensive coordinator at St. Thomas Aquinas High School in [south] Florida."

Spare time? What little Carter enjoys these days is devoted to family and his hobbies.

"My wife, Melanie, and I have been married for 16 years, and she was a graduate of Ohio State. We have two children, Duron and Monterae, and they are 15 and 12," he said. "I love playing golf, and I love going to big sporting events—golf, basketball, or football."

The self-styled bottom line on Carter the Buckeye goes like this: "I want people to know how much I enjoyed playing football for OSU. The first time I ran on the field, it was an experience that I will never forget, that will never leave me. The reaction of the student body [and] the whole crowd; it was addictive and not like anything I had ever experienced. Mike [Lanese], my roommate, always warned me. He tried to tell me what it was going to be like. But I didn't think it would be any different from high school. I had played for a big school, played in many big games, and thought I had seen a lot. But the first time I ran on that field, in my three years of playing at Ohio State and my 16 years of playing in the NFL, I never experienced that initial rush again—and I was always in pursuit of that initial feeling."

35

JASON SIMMONS

BIRTH DATE: December 20, 1970
HOMETOWN: Akron, Ohio
RESIDENCE: Huber Heights, Ohio
POSITION: Defensive end
HEIGHT: 6-foot-5
WEIGHT: 240 pounds
YEARS: 1990 to 1993

Simmons didn't play football until his freshman year at St. Vincent/St. Mary High School in Akron. ... He broke (ex-OSU linebacker) Eric Kumerow's all-time career sack record, ending with 27.5. He set a Buckeyes record with 50 career tackles for a loss. ... Simmons led the Buckeyes to a share of the 1993 Big Ten title and John Cooper's first trip to a bowl game as OSU coach. ... He was a highly competitive defensive end with excellent pass-rushing skills, which he used with the St. Louis Rams, the Kansas City Chiefs, the Hamilton Tiger-Cats of the Canadian Football League and the Scottish Claymores of NFL Europe. Originally, he was signed as a free agent by the Washington Redskins.

Jason Simmons became something of a sack master at Ohio State.

The Run-up

Drew Bledsoe and the Washington State Cougars came to play on a warm, sunny day. For the Buckeyes, it was an important non-conference game. They had the opportunity to go 3-0 for the first time under coach John Cooper, and people were coming to see all-everything sophomore quarterback Bledsoe.

"On game day, one of my favorite pregame traditions was driving the bus through campus with all the tailgaters honking and the crowd cheering," Simmons says. "Everyone was excited to see us. We did our set D-line pregame routine working on basic blocking schemes and then moved over to work with the O-line on some pass rush drills."

Simmons didn't expect to see much of Bledsoe, but he made the most of his chance. Perhaps it could be couched this way: Baptism by fire.

The Game

By Jason Simmons

Washington State at Ohio State—September 21, 1991

As a red-shirt freshman playing behind John Kacherski the year before, I wasn't scheduled to get much playing time, but John blew out his knee in the second quarter of the first game, and I ended up playing the rest of the year.

John came back the next year strong and healthy. Having played so much the previous year, I had increased expectations for myself; however, he was a senior, a co-captain (in 1991) and he worked his tail off, so he started, and I backed him up. I was disappointed, having started the previous year, but was behind him 100 percent. I knew I would get my chance.

John and I were good friends. He was the first person to come over and congratulate me each time. And that's what made it so great.

The competition did not get personal. We were happy for each other to succeed and just wanted the team to win.

The Aftermath

Simmons made four of the defense's nine sacks in the 33-19 win, set the school's single-game record, and then received some good news the next day.

"I didn't realize I had set a record until the following day when I ran into Coach Cooper at Bob Evans, and he told me congratulations on the record," he said. "That was a pretty amazing feeling."

Simmons still is in football, coaching the Northmont High School defensive line in Clayton (just north of Dayton). He is an intervention specialist for eighth graders with learning disabilities at Northmont Middle School. He also coaches the high school's track team.

Jason has been married to Colleen for more than 11 years. They have a son, Hunter, and a daughter, Graysen. In his spare time, Simmons either is outside hunting and fishing or inside doing woodworking.

Simmons looks back with satisfaction at his OSU days, knowing he left it all on the field.

"I was in one of those star-studded recruiting classes, and as an offensive lineman-defensive tackle, I felt like I was an afterthought with that class," he said. "I was not one of the biggest, strongest, or fastest, but I worked hard and outworked everyone. I made sure to give 100 percent all the time."

36

STAN WHITE

BIRTH DATE: October 24, 1949
HOMETOWN: Kent, Ohio
RESIDENCE: Baltimore, Maryland
POSITION: Linebacker
HEIGHT: 6-foot-1
WEIGHT: 224 pounds
YEARS: 1969 to 1971

White made All-State in football, basketball and baseball. ... His son, Stan White Jr., is a fullback-tight end at Ohio State. ... His daughters, Amanda and Meghan, have had considerable success in cross-country and track. ... He played 13 years in the NFL with the Detroit Lions and Baltimore Colts.

The Run-up

Bo Schembechler made a big splash in 1969—his first year as Michigan head coach. His Wolverines upset Ohio State, 24-12, and Woody Hayes drove Stan White and his teammates relentlessly for the next year.

"That game had been my first bad experience at Michigan stadium," he said. "Woody had that 24-12 score plastered everywhere in our facility. Every day, when we went out to practice, we walked across the mat that said 24-12 on it. We practiced against Michigan all spring."

The coaches and players weren't the only ones eager for kickoff.

"It was the loudest crowd I'd ever heard," White added. "Both teams entered the game undefeated. In those days, only the winner would be going to a bowl game—there weren't any other bowl games like today. Woody had to take us out of the dorms the week before because the kids were so riled up, they'd come by and chant Jack Tatum's name. They put us in the Fawcett Center to live. It was the most intense week in my football career, and I played for 13 years in the NFL after that. There was nothing like that week.

"Plus, it was the last game in Ohio Stadium for the [former] Super Sophomores, guys like Rex Kern and Jack Tatum. It was fever pitch all week long. There was never more emotion in a game then the preparation for that game that I've been through."

The Game

By Stan White

Michigan at Ohio State—November 21, 1970

After we stormed out on the field, and I kicked off, Rick Ferko hit the Michigan guy, and he fumbled. We recovered on around the 25-yard line. This was the opening play. The crowd just erupted. It was

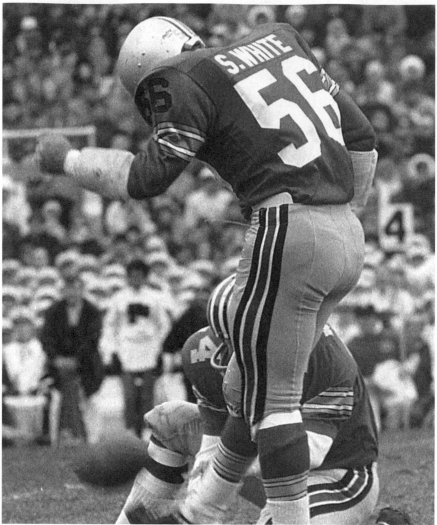

Offense or defense, it didn't matter. Stan White was a contributor in multiple phases of the game.

unbelievable. We had all this pent-up emotion. Everyone in the stands was screaming.

We went in and got a field goal out of that. So immediately, it was 3-0. I think they tied it up 3-3 at one point. Then we went ahead 10-3 when Rex hit Bruce Jankowski with a touchdown. They came in and scored to make it 10-9; then Tim Anderson came in and blocked the extra point. Then Fred Schram kicked a field goal to make it 13-9.

Then I kicked off into the end zone, and they took it at the 20. They threw a pass, which I intercepted and ran back to the 9-yard line. This was the only time in the 21 years that I played football that I ever heard the crowd in the middle of a play. When the people in the stadium saw I was going to intercept the pass, they completely exploded, and I could hear it before I even made the play. I went down the left hash mark and tried to go outside. OSU middle guard Jim Stillwagon slipped and fell down in front of me, and I had to cut to the inside. I ran to the 9-yard line and held on to the ball for dear life. It was in the middle of the fourth quarter. Three plays later, we scored a touchdown, making it 20-9, which was the winning margin.

I was on defense, and they were the No. 1-rushing team in the country—we held them to 37 yards rushing. We stopped them completely from running the football. We were so focused on the game.

The Aftermath

White got a taste of celebrity after the game, which he has never forgotten.

"When the clock ran out, everyone stormed on the field," he said. "We never talked to the press, except after the Michigan game, so that was one of my first interviews because I had made the interception. Somewhere I have a picture from after the game of a wire photo of me being interviewed in the locker room.

"It was a great time. They closed down High Street after the game, and we went up there and had a great time for about the next 12 hours after that."

It wasn't just about the cameras and parties, however.

"I remember going back to an accounting class, and Ray Kraznuski, the professor, had me stand up and had the class applaud. It was a fun time, we were going to the Rose Bowl, we had beaten Michigan—it was all that you could want at the time."

After OSU, Stan went on to a very productive NFL career in Baltimore and Detroit. When football was over, he put his law degree to good use as an attorney in Baltimore for Samuel James Ltd., a financial firm.

His family is his pride and joy, however.

"I have a daughter, Amanda, who went to Stanford. She won the Dial Award for the outstanding scholar-athlete in the country," White beamed. "She was a national high school cross-country champion. She was also an Olympic trials swimmer. She was a professional tri-athlete until she had her third little boy, when she decided to retire.

"My other daughter, Meghan, is also a runner. She won the Wendy's high school award for the state of Maryland. She went to [the University of] North Carolina.

"Stan Jr. is a red-shirt junior, but is finishing his first year of his MBA at Ohio State, where he is a fullback and plays a little tight end. He finished his undergrad in three years.

"My wife is Patty, who I met at Ohio State. She checked everyone in at the commons where we ate. Everyone wanted to be friends with her so we could get a second meal on steak night. Everyone made friends with her, and I ended up going out with her. We've been married 33 years."

White coaches at Baltimore's Gilman School, which was ranked No. 12 in the nation last year by *USA Today*. Two of White's former players started for Notre Dame in the 2006 Fiesta Bowl, in which OSU beat the Fighting Irish, 34-20.

While White has justifiable pride in his college and pro football accomplishments, he said his kids are his legacy. "I'd like to be remembered as the father of Stan White Jr.," he said. "I think that's how I'm remembered now. I remember when I went from being Stan White of the Baltimore Colts, to Stan White, Amanda's father when she was having all of her success, and then Meghan's dad, and now Stan's."

Celebrate the Heroes of Ohio State Sports
and College Sports in These Other Releases from Sports Publishing!

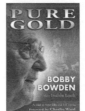